2nd Edition

Last Will & Testament Kit

EstateBee

By EstateBee Publishing

A Special Request – Please Leave a Review on Amazon

Thank you for purchasing this Last Will & Testament Kit.

Your positive book review could really help us and help other customers make informed decisions when purchasing self-help kits like this one.

This link will take you to the Amazon.co.uk review page for this book. We would be very grateful if you could please leave a positive 5 Star Review.

Estate-bee.com/review30

Bibliographic Data

- International Standard Book Number (ISBN): 978-1-913889-18-0
- Printed in the United States of America
- First Edition: July 2012
- Second Edition: October 2021

Published By: EstateBee Limited
                        23 Lynn Road
                        London SW12 9LB
                        United Kingdom

Printed and Distributed By: Kindle Direct Publishing, an Amazon Company

For more information, e-mail books@estate-bee.com.

Copyright

Trademarks

All terms mentioned in this kit that are known to be trademarks or service marks have been appropriately capitalized. Use of a term in this kit should not be regarded as affecting the validity of any trademark or service mark.

Warning and Disclaimer

Although precautions have been taken in preparing this kit, neither the publisher nor the author assumes any responsibility for errors or omissions. No warranty of fitness is implied, and all implied warranties are excluded to the fullest extent permitted by law. The information is provided on an "as is" basis. Neither the author nor the publisher shall be liable or responsible to any person or entity for any loss or damages (whether arising by negligence or otherwise) arising from the use of or reliance on the information contained in this kit or from the use of any forms or documents accompanying it.

Important Note

This kit is meant as a general guide to preparing your own last will and testament. While effort has been made to make this kit as accurate as possible, laws and their interpretation are constantly changing. As such, you are advised to update this information with your own research and/or counsel and to consult with your personal legal, financial, and/or medical advisors before acting on any information contained in this kit.

This kit is not meant to provide legal, financial, or medical advice or to create any solicitor-client or other advisory relationship. The authors and publisher shall have neither liability (whether in negligence or otherwise) nor responsibility to any person or entity with respect to any loss or damage caused or alleged to be caused directly or indirectly by the information contained in this kit or the use of that information.

About EstateBee

EstateBee, the international self-help legal publisher, was founded in 2000 by lawyers from one of the most prestigious international law firms in the World.

Our aim was simple - to provide access to quality legal information and products at an affordable price.

Our will writing software was first published in that year and, following its adaptation to cater for the legal systems of various countries worldwide, quickly drew more than 40,000 visitors per month to our website. From this humble start, EstateBee has quickly grown to become a leading international estate planning and asset protection self-help publisher with legal titles in the United States, Canada, the United Kingdom, Australia, and Ireland.

Our publications provide customers with the confidence and knowledge to help them deal with everyday estate planning issues such as the preparation of a last will and testament, a living trust, a power of attorney, administering an estate and much more.

By providing customers with much needed information and forms, we enable them to place themselves in a position where they can protect both themselves and their families using easy to read legal documents and forward planning techniques.

The Future....

We are always seeking to expand and improve the products and services we offer. However, to do this, we need to hear from interested authors and to receive feedback from our customers.

If something isn't clear to you in one of our publications, please let us know and we'll try to make it clearer in the next edition. If you can't find the answer you want and have a suggestion for an addition to our range, we'll happily look at that too.

Using Self-Help Kits

Before using a self-help kit, you need to carefully consider the advantages and disadvantages of doing so – particularly where the subject matter is of a legal or tax related nature.

In writing our self-help kits, we try to provide readers with an overview of the laws in a specific area, as well as some sample documents. While this overview is often general in nature, it provides a good starting point for those wishing to carry out a more detailed review of a topic.

However, unlike a solicitor advising a client, we cannot cover every conceivable eventuality that might affect our readers. Within the intended scope of this kit, we can only cover the principal areas in each topic, and even where we cover these areas, we can still only do so to a moderate extent. To do otherwise would result in the writing of a textbook which would be capable of use by legal professionals. This is not what we do.

We try to present useful information and documents that can be used by an average reader with little or no legal knowledge. While our sample documents can be used in most cases, everybody's personal circumstances are different. As such, they may not be suitable for everyone. You may have personal circumstances which might impact the effectiveness of these documents or even your desire to use them. The reality is that without engaging a solicitor to review your personal circumstances, this risk will always exist. It's for this very reason that you need to consider whether the cost of using a do-it-yourself legal document outweighs the risk that there may be something special about your circumstances which might not be taken into account by the sample documents attached to this kit (or indeed any other sample documents).

It goes without saying (we hope) that if you are in any doubt as to whether the documents in this kit are suitable for use in your circumstances, you should contact a suitably qualified solicitor for advice before using them. Remember the decision to use these documents is yours. We are not advising you in any respect.

In using this kit, you should also consider the fact that this kit has been written with the purpose of providing a general overview of the laws in Canada. As such, it does not attempt to cover all the various procedural nuances and specific requirements that may apply – although we do point some of these out along the way. Rather, in our kit, we try to provide forms which give a fair example of the type of forms which are commonly used in Canada. Nevertheless, it remains possible that some specific requirements have not been taken into account in our forms.

Another thing that you should remember is that the law changes – thousands of new laws are brought into force every day, and, by the same token, thousands are repealed or amended every day. As such, it is possible that while you are reading this kit, the law might well have been changed. We hope it hasn't, but the chance does exist. To address this, when we become aware of them, we do send updates to our customers about material changes to the law. We also ensure that our books are reviewed and revised regularly to take account of these changes.

Anyway, assuming that all the above is acceptable to you, let's move on to exploring the topic at hand.........last will and testaments.

Table of Contents

Introduction to Wills

Introduction

In this kit, we will give you a brief introduction to wills as well as the laws relating to wills in Canada. After we've done that, we'll take you step-by-step through the process of making your own will. If you already have a firm understanding of wills, you can skip straight to this section and make your will – although we do recommend that you read the information in this kit first before making your will.

What is a Will?

Simply put, a will is a legal document that allows you to express your desires and intentions regarding the distribution of your property following your death. It is your will that sets out how, when and even why you want your property apportioned between your relatives, friends and charities when you die. As the author of your will, you will be known as the 'testator' if you are male and as the 'testatrix' if you are female.

Types of Wills

There are five main types of will recognised as legal in Canada.

(i) A *conventional will* is one which has been signed by the testator in the presence of two witnesses who, in turn, sign their name in the presence of the testator.

(ii) A *holograph will* is one which has been written entirely in the handwriting of the testator and is usually signed at the bottom of the will. Holograph wills are legal in Alberta, Manitoba and Saskatchewan. They are not recognised as legal in any other provinces in Canada.

(iii) A *notarial will* is a type of will which has been signed by the testator in the presence of a witness and a notary public. They are most commonly used in Quebec. In the normal case, the notary will retain the original will and issue notarized copies to the testator. Notarial wills are usually exempt from the formalities of probate.

(iv) A *self-proving will* is a will which is presented to the probate court as part of the probate process. In the normal course, if there is any doubt as to the authenticity of the signature of the testator appearing on a will, the court may call upon the persons who witnessed the execution of the will to certify in court that the signature of the testator appearing on the will is in fact authentic and that the will was validly executed. One way of avoiding having to call these witnesses to court is to pre-validate the testator's signature. To do this, both the testator and the witnesses sign a document called a 'self-proving affidavit'. This is little more than a document in which the witnesses acknowledge that they witnessed the testator sign the will. However, the big difference is that it is signed in the presence of a notary who, in turn, officially seals the document to give it authenticity. The court will normally accept the execution of a will with an accompanying affidavit as genuine. The affidavit, when attached to the related will, is called a 'self-proving will'. Self proving-wills are common in Alberta and Quebec.

(v) An 'international will' is recognized in each of Alberta, Manitoba, Ontario, New Brunswick, Newfoundland, Nova Scotia, Prince Edward Island and Saskatchewan. It requires the testator to make the will in the presence of two witnesses and in the presence of a qualified lawyer.

Why Make a Will?

There are many benefits to making a will and very few drawbacks. Perhaps the biggest benefit is that it allows you to dictate, via a clear legal document, how you want your assets distributed following your death. This is particularly important if you are married or have children as, in each case, you will no doubt want to provide appropriately for your loved ones. In the absence of having a will, the 'rules of intestacy' (which apply where a person dies without making a will) will determine how your assets are distributed amongst your heirs. As the definition of 'heirs' only includes family members, this distribution may not be in accordance with your wishes.

Did You Know

Over 280,000 Canadians die every year (Source: Statistics Canada). It is estimated that 85% of these Canadians die without having prepared a will.

Another good reason for making a will is that it allows you to appoint someone as your executor. Your executor is the person or persons who will be responsible for carrying out the instructions in your will and for tidying up your affairs after you die. If you don't appoint an executor in your will, the rules of intestacy will determine who fulfils that role. The person appointed under these rules may not be someone that you would wish to have trawling through your affairs.

Wills also allow you to appoint guardians to take care of your minor children and to make property management arrangements to cater for young beneficiaries who will inherit under your will. We'll discuss guardians and property management in more detail in the ensuing pages.

Intestacy & What Happens Without a Will

When a person dies without making a will or if their will cannot be located, is deemed false or invalid (for not meeting the statutory requirements described below), it's called dying intestate. Each province has a set of statutory rules governing who is entitled to receive a person's property if they die intestate in that province. These rules are commonly known as the 'rules of intestacy' or the 'rules of intestate succession'.

Quite often, the application of the rules of intestacy result in the distribution of a deceased person's property in a manner that they would never have wanted. This is because the rules set out a list of people (known as 'heirs') who are entitled to receive shares in the deceased's property; as well as the amount of these shares and the order in which they are entitled to receive them.

In an intestacy situation, the first beneficiaries to receive the deceased's property are usually the surviving spouse and then the children of the deceased. However, if there is no surviving spouse or children, then the general rule of thumb is that the bigger the estate is, the more distant the relatives who will inherit part of it. Such beneficiaries might include the deceased's grandchildren, parents, siblings, grandparents, nieces and nephews, cousins and so on. In those rare cases where no relatives can be found the deceased's property will revert to the provincial government's treasury.

Did You Know

Your estate is the total sum of your possessions, property and money held in your name (minus your debts) at the time of your death.

Distribution of Estate on Intestacy

The amount of a deceased person's estate that each heir is entitled to receive on intestacy in each province is broadly set out in the tables below.

Alberta	
Survived by Spouse Only	All to spouse.
Survived by Spouse and Relatives, but no Children	All to spouse.
Survived by Child or Children Only	All to children (**1**).
Survived by Spouse and One Child	If both the deceased and the spouse are parents of the child, then all goes to spouse. If the deceased and the spouse are not both parents of the child, then the spouse gets the higher of (a) $150,000 and (b) 50% of the deceased's estate; and the rest goes to the child (**1**).

Survived by Spouse and Children	If both the deceased and the spouse are parents of all the children, then all goes to the spouse. If the deceased and the spouse are not both parents of the children, then the spouse gets the higher of (a) $150,000 and (b) 50% of the deceased's estate; and the rest goes to the children **(1)**.
Survived by No Spouse and No Children	All to the closest next of kin; usually in the following order: parents, if none survive then to siblings (8), if none survive then to nieces and nephews, if none survive then to more remote next of kin. If none survive or none can be located, all goes to the provincial government.
Definition of Spouse and Children	Spouse includes an adult interdependent partner of not less than three years or someone who cohabited in a relationship of some permanence with the deceased if there is a child of the relationship, but excludes spouses that are separated.

British Columbia	
Survived by Spouse Only	All to spouse.
Survived by Spouse and Relatives, but no Children	All to spouse.
Survived by Child or Children Only	All to children **(1)**.
Survived by Spouse and One Child	If both the deceased and the spouse are parents of the child, the first $300,000 goes to the spouse **(3)** and the rest is split equally between the spouse and child **(1)**. If both are not parents of the child, the first $150,000 goes to the spouse **(3)** and the rest is split equally between the spouse and child **(1)**.
Survived by Spouse and Children	If both the deceased and the spouse are parents of all the children, the first $300,000 goes to the spouse **(3)** and the rest is split equally between the spouse and children **(1)**. If both are not parents of all the children, the first $150,000 goes to the spouse **(3)** and the rest is split equally between the spouse and children **(1)**.

Survived by No Spouse and No Children	As above.
Definition of Spouse and Children	Spouse includes an adult interdependent partner or partners in a marriage-like relationship for two years prior to death, but excludes (in most cases) separated spouses.

Manitoba	
Survived by Spouse Only	All to spouse.
Survived by Spouse and Relatives, but no Children	All to spouse.
Survived by Child or Children Only	All to children (1).
Survived by Spouse and One Child	All goes to the spouse where the child is also a child of the surviving spouse (5), or if not, the spouse gets the greater of $50,000 or ½ of the deceased's estate (10); and the rest is split ½ to the spouse and ½ to the child (6).
Survived by Spouse and Children	All goes to the spouse where all the children also children of the surviving spouse (5), or if not, the spouse gets the greater of $50,000 or ½ of the deceased's estate (10); and the rest is split ½ to the spouse and ½ to the children (6).
Survived by No Spouse and No Children	As set out for Alberta
Definition of Spouse and Children	Spouse includes common-law partners who registered their relationship under The Vital Statistics Act, or cohabited in a conjugal relationship either for a period of three years, or for a period of one year while raising a child. Includes separated spouses who had not previously divided their assets under a separation agreement.

Newfoundland

Survived by Spouse Only	All to spouse.
Survived by Spouse and Relatives, but no Children	All to spouse.
Survived by Child or Children Only	All to children **(1)**.
Survived by Spouse and One Child	1/2 goes to the spouse and 1/2 goes to the child **(1)**.
Survived by Spouse and Children	1/3 goes to the spouse and 2/3 goes to the children **(1)**.
Survived by No Spouse and No Children	As set out for Alberta.
Definition of Spouse and Children	Spouse only includes legally married spouses. "Child" does not include a stepchild.

New Brunswick	
Survived by Spouse Only	All to spouse.
Survived by Spouse and Relatives, but no Children	All to spouse.
Survived by Child or Children Only	All to children **(1)**.
Survived by Spouse and One Child	Marital property goes to the spouse, and the rest of the deceased's estate is split equally between the spouse and child **(1)**.
Survived by Spouse and Children	Marital property goes to the spouse, and the rest of the deceased's estate is split equally between the spouse and children **(1)**.
Survived by No Spouse and No Children	As set out for Alberta.

Definition of Spouse and Children	Includes legally married spouses only. Children does not include stepchildren.

Northwest Territories	
Survived by Spouse Only	All to spouse.
Survived by Spouse and Relatives, but no Children	All to spouse.
Survived by Child or Children Only	All to children (1).
Survived by Spouse and One Child	First $50,000 goes to the spouse, and the rest of the estate is split equally between the spouse and child.
Survived by Spouse and Children	First $50,000 goes to the spouse (2), and the rest of the estate is split 1/3 to the spouse and 2/3 to the children (1).
Survived by No Spouse and No Children	As set out for Alberta.
Definition of Spouse and Children	Spouse includes common-law partners who had cohabited for a period of at least two years, or had cohabited in a relationship of some permanence and were together the natural or adoptive parents of a child. It excludes legally married spouses who were cohabiting with someone else at the date of death, had initiated divorce proceedings and had not reconciled, or had previously divided their assets on separation. "Child" does not include a stepchild.

Nova Scotia	
Survived by Spouse Only	All to spouse.
Survived by Spouse and Relatives, but no Children	All to spouse.
Survived by Child or Children Only	All to children (1).

Survived by Spouse and One Child	First $50,000 goes to the spouse, and the rest of the deceased's estate is split equally between the spouse and child **(2)**.
Survived by Spouse and Children	First $50,000 goes to the spouse **(2)**, the rest of the deceased's estate is split 1/3 to the spouse and 2/3 to the children **(1)**.
Survived by No Spouse and No Children	As set out for Alberta.
Definition of Spouse and Children	Includes legally married spouses and cohabiting partners. Spouse may claim matrimonial home regardless of share of estate. "Child" does not include a stepchild, or a child raised by a non-biological parent that has not been legally adopted.

Nunavut	
Survived by Spouse Only	All to spouse.
Survived by Spouse and Relatives, but no Children	All to spouse.
Survived by Child or Children Only	All to children **(1)**.
Survived by Spouse and One Child	First $50,000 goes to the spouse, and the rest of the estate is split equally between the spouse and child (1).
Survived by Spouse and Children	First $50,000 goes to the spouse (2), and the rest of the estate is split 1/3 to the spouse and 2/3 to the children **(1)**.
Survived by No Spouse and No Children	As set out for Alberta.
Definition of Spouse and Children	As set out for Northwest Territories.

Ontario	
Survived by Spouse Only	All to spouse.

Survived by Spouse and Relatives, but no Children	All to spouse.
Survived by Child or Children Only	All to children **(1)**.
Survived by Spouse and One Child	First $200,000 goes to the spouse, and the rest is split equally between the spouse and child **(1) (4)**.
Survived by Spouse and Children	First $200,000 goes to the spouse, and 1/3 of the rest goes to spouse; with 2/3 going to the children **(1) (4)**.
Survived by No Spouse and No Children	As set out for Alberta.
Definition of Spouse and Children	Includes married spouses only. Spouse may opt for an equalization payment under s. 5 of the Family Law Act, if it results in a greater share of the deceased's estate.

Prince Edward Island	
Survived by Spouse Only	All to spouse.
Survived by Spouse and Relatives, but no Children	All to spouse.
Survived by Child or Children Only	All to children **(1)**.
Survived by Spouse and One Child	1/2 goes to the spouse and 1/2 goes to the child **(1)**.
Survived by Spouse and Children	1/3 goes to the spouse and 2/3 goes to the children **(1)**.
Survived by No Spouse and No Children	As set out for Alberta.
Definition of Spouse and Children	Spouse only includes legally married spouses. "Child" does not include a stepchild.

Quebec	
Survived by Spouse Only	All to spouse.
Survived by Spouse and Relatives, but no Children	If the deceased is survived by both a spouse and parents, then 2/3 goes to the spouse, and 1/3 to surviving parent(s). If both parents are deceased, their 1/3 share goes to the deceased's siblings (9).
Survived by Child or Children Only	All to children (1).
Survived by Spouse and One Child	1/3 goes to the spouse (7), 2/3 go to the child (1).
Survived by Spouse and Children	1/3 goes to the spouse (7), 2/3 go to the children (1).
Survived by No Spouse and No Children	As set out for Alberta.
Definition of Spouse and Children	Spouse includes those in a civil union.

Saskatchewan	
Survived by Spouse Only	All to spouse.
Survived by Spouse and Relatives, but no Children	All to spouse.
Survived by Child or Children Only	All to children (1).
Survived by Spouse and One Child	First $100,000 goes to the spouse, and the rest is split equally between the spouse and child (1).
Survived by Spouse and Children	First $100,000 goes to the spouse. 1/3 of the rest goes to the spouse, and 2/3 goes to the children equally (1).

Survived by No Spouse and No Children	As set out for Alberta.
Definition of Spouse and Children	Spouse includes common-law partners who cohabited with the deceased as a spouse continuously for a period of not less than two years; and at the date of death were either cohabiting with the deceased, or had ceased to cohabitate within two years of the date of death. It excludes legally married spouses who were cohabiting with someone else at the date of death.

Yukon	
Survived by Spouse Only	All to spouse.
Survived by Spouse and Relatives, but no Children	All to spouse.
Survived by Child or Children Only	All to children **(1)**.
Survived by Spouse and One Child	First $75,000 goes to the spouse, and the rest of the estate is split equally between the spouse and child **(1)**.
Survived by Spouse and Children	First $75,000 goes to the spouse **(2)**, and the rest is split 1/3 to the spouse and 2/3 to the children **(1)**.
Survived by No Spouse and No Children	As set out for Alberta.
Definition of Spouse and Children	Common-law spouses may apply to the court for a share of the estate. "Child" does not include a stepchild.

Notes:

1. Per stirpes rule (further details below) applies.
2. Spouse may take the house and contents instead of the $50,000 / $75,000.
3. Spouse also takes household furniture and a life interest (right to live) in the family home.
4. Subject to a possible equalization claim under provincial legislation.
5. If all the children are also children of the surviving spouse.

6. Children of deceased child (grandchildren) share in the estate.

7. Subject to provincial legislation.

8. Children of deceased brothers and sisters share their parent's share.

9. Depends on who the other survivors are, so this may vary slightly.

10. Spouse may claim a life interest in the family home plus a possible equalization payment under provincial legislation.

Did You Know

A life interest is a right that is granted to someone for their lifetime – such as a right to reside in a particular house. When the recipient of that right dies, the right dies with them.

Children and the Per Stirpes Rule

Fortunately, for most children, the law treats legitimate and illegitimate children in the same way when it comes to intestacy. As such, they are both generally entitled to share in their deceased parent's estate on intestacy. However, the law treat's stepchildren differently. In many instances, unless they are legally adopted by the deceased, stepchildren will have no automatic right to receive anything on intestacy from a deceased stepparent. For this reason, it's important to make specific provision for them in your will – especially if they have not been formally adopted.

When it comes to children, the 'per stirpes' rule can apply in certain instances. This rule provides that if a beneficiary/heir predeceases the testator/intestate leaving a child, then that child takes the share that his or her parent would have been entitled to receive had they been alive. Where there is more than one child, the parent's share is divided equally amongst the children. However, when we talk about children in this instance, it should be remembered that stepchildren may not be entitled to benefit under this rule.

Common Law Spouses and Partners

References to spouses and partners in the tables above are references to legal spouses and partners only and do not include common law spouses or partners. As the law often does not recognise the rights of common law spouses or partners to benefit from the estate of their deceased partner, it is important to ensure that they are expressly included in your will if you want them to benefit. Otherwise, there is a real risk that they will end up with nothing on an intestacy.

Did You Know

The definition of 'spouse', and with it the succession rights of common law partners and same sex partners, continues to evolve in Canada. Many provinces now recognise the rights of these individuals to receive an element of their deceased partner's estate on intestacy. In Quebec, for example, partners (both opposite and same sex partners) who have entered into a civil union are now entitled to a share of their deceased partner's estate on intestacy. Similarly, registered domestic partners in Nova Scotia are treated as 'spouses' for the purposes of intestate succession and spousal rights on death. In Alberta, partners in a registered adult interdependent partnership have also been afforded certain spousal rights. However, making a will and leaving express gifts to your partner is arguably the best way to ensure that your partner benefits from your estate following your death. If you have any questions about your partner's rights on intestacy, speak to your solicitor.

Partial Intestacy

In addition to providing for situations where a person has died without making a will, the rules of intestacy also provide for situations where a person fails to dispose of all of their property under their will. This is called a "partial intestacy". A partial intestacy commonly occurs where a will fails to include what's known as a 'residuary' clause in their will. A residuary clause simply provides that any of the deceased's property which has not been expressly gifted to someone under the terms of their will is to be given to a named beneficiary or beneficiaries known as the residuary beneficiary/beneficiaries. A partial intestacy can also occur where the residuary beneficiary or beneficiaries die(s) before the testator and no alternate beneficiaries are named to receive the residue of the estate in their place. Where a partial intestacy occurs, any property not covered under the will is distributed in accordance with the rules of intestacy outlined above.

Appointment of Guardians by the Court

Any parent who has parental responsibility for a minor child should consider appointing a guardian to look after the child if they (and the child's other parent or guardian, if any) are unable to care for them due to death, incapacity or otherwise. There are two primary ways of appointing a guardian. Firstly, a formal guardianship agreement can be signed between the parent and the prospective guardian that formally provides for the guardianship arrangement. Alternatively, a clause can be inserted in a will appointing a guardian for the testator's child or children. This latter method is much more common than the former.

If you don't use any of these methods to appoint a guardian, provincial laws will determine who takes care of your minor children following your death. In many cases, the Public Trustee will become responsible for the management of your minor children's assets. In turn, the provincial child welfare services will become responsible for the welfare, health and education of your minor children. A relative or another person with a connection to the children can make an application to the court to be appointed as guardian of the children instead of the Public Trustee or child welfare services. Where such an application is made, the court will consider the application having regard to what it considers to be in the best interest of the children. It will then make a determination regarding their ongoing guardianship.

Appointment of Administrator by the Court

Finally, if you don't make a will, the rules of intestacy will determine who will act as the administrator of your estate. The administrator of your estate performs a similar function to an executor in that they collect, safeguard and distribute your estate following your death. Generally, if none of your close relatives apply to act as administrator, the provincial government will get involved in the administration of your estate through the appointment of the Public Trustee or the official administrator.

It may also be necessary for the administrator to take out an 'administrator bond'. This is a type of insurance bond which is taken out to compensate the estate in the event that its value is depleted due to mismanagement by the administrator. Where such a bond is taken out, the cost will be payable by your estate. This will reduce the value of your overall estate which will pass to your heirs.

Can I Make My Own Will?

Absolutely! Provided your estate is not too complex (and most estates are not complex) and you are not actively trying to disinherit your spouse or child, you can easily make your own will. While many lawyers will correctly tell you that it's important to get proper legal advice when making a will, the reality is that most of them use simple template or precedent will forms for the vast majority of their clients. These are the same type of templates that are included with this kit. It most cases, all you need to do to prepare your own will is to decide on a few simple matters like who you want to gift your property to, who you want to act as your executor, who you want to act as guardian of your children and who you want to act as witnesses to the execution of your will.

However, when making your will, you should pay close attention to the rights of spouses and children which will be discussed below. In this respect, if you wish to disinherit them in any manner, you should speak to a lawyer. Similarly, if your estate is large or complex (such as where you own a business or have large agricultural holdings) you should obtain legal and tax advice.

How to Make a Valid Will

Each province has laws which set out the minimum requirements for a conventional will to be valid in that province. In general, in order for a will to be valid, it must:

- be made by a person who has reached the age of majority in their province;

- be made by a person voluntarily and without pressure from any other person;

- be made by a person who is of 'sound and disposing mind';

- be in writing;

- be signed by the testator in the presence of at least two witnesses;

- be signed by the witnesses in the presence of the testator (after he or she has signed it) and in the presence of each other. A beneficiary under the will or the spouse or interdependent partner of such a beneficiary should not act as a witness to the signing of the will. If they do, the gift to the beneficiary under the will shall be deemed to be invalid, although the will itself will remain valid; and

- include an attestation (signing) clause.

If the above requirements are not complied with, the will may be deemed to be invalid - in which case the rules of intestacy will apply.

Age of Majority

The age of majority is a legal description that denotes the threshold age at which a person ceases to be a minor and subsequently becomes legally responsible for his or her own actions and decisions. It is the age at which the responsibility of the minor's parents or guardians over them is relinquished. Reaching the age of majority also has a number of important practical consequences for the minor. The minor is now legally entitled to do certain things which he or she could not legally do before. For example, he or she is now legally entitled to enter into binding contracts, hold significant assets, buy stocks and shares, vote in elections, buy and/or consume alcohol, and so on. But more importantly from an estate planning perspective, the minor can now make a will.

The chart below demonstrates the age of majority as defined by each province.

Age of Majority by Province			
Province	**Age of Majority**	**Province**	**Age of Majority**
Alberta	18	Nunavut	19
British Columbia	19	Ontario	18
Manitoba	18	Prince Edward Island	18
New Brunswick	19	Quebec	18
Newfoundland and Labrador	19	Saskatchewan	18
Northwest Territories	19	Yukon Territories	19
Nova Scotia	19		

It is a general rule that a person must reach the age of majority in their province before being entitled to make a valid legal will. There are however some exceptions to this general rule. Typically, a person under the age of eighteen years who is already married, or who has been married, is deemed of sufficient age to execute a will or a codicil. Similarly, an underage person who joins the military or is on active military service can also make a will or a codicil, as can a seaman or naval officer at sea.

Mental Capacity and Undue Influence

In order to make a valid legal will, you must typically be of 'sound disposing mind'. 'Sound disposing mind' is generally taken to mean someone who understands:

- what a will is;
- that they are making a will;
- the general extent of their property;
- who their heirs and family members are; and
- the way in which their will proposes to distribute their property (and, of course, to be satisfied with that.)

It is important to note that you need to be of sound disposing mind when you execute your will, not immediately prior to your death. As such, if you end up suffering from any kind of mental impairment late in life such as dementia or Alzheimer's disease, or even from an addiction to drugs or alcohol, the court will look at your mental state at the time you executed your will in order to determine whether it was validly made. If it can be shown that you were not mentally impaired or under the influence at the time you executed your will, the court will most likely deem the will to be valid. If you are suffering from any such impairments, it is advisable that you visit your doctor on the day you execute your will (or even execute it in your doctor's presence) and have your doctor prepare a medical certificate stating that in his or her professional opinion you were mentally competent and lucid at the time you executed your will. These types of statements generally have a strong persuasive effect on the courts, which typically tend to concede mental lucidity in such cases.

Another form of mental incapacity comes under the heading 'undue influence'. Undue influence is the exertion by a third party in a position of trust or authority of any kind of control or influence over another person such that the other person signs a contract or other legal instrument (such as a mortgage or deed) which, absent the influence of the third party, he or she would not ordinarily have signed. A contract or legal instrument may be set aside as being non-binding on any party who signs it while under undue influence.

Claims of undue influence are often raised by sibling beneficiaries in circumstances where one sibling is bequeathed more from a parent than the others. In making your will, you must therefore be careful to avoid potential claims of undue influence where you leave more to one of your children than another. Any such suggestion would give an aggrieved beneficiary the opportunity to attack and try to overturn the terms of your will. In order to reduce the potential likelihood of such claims, it's often useful to document the reasons why you are leaving more to one child than another. Your note can then be attached to your will or at least kept with it.

A second scenario in which claims for undue influence are often raised arises where a testator uses a beneficiary's lawyer to draft their will. In such circumstances, aggrieved beneficiaries will, in reliance on that very fact, often assert that the use of the beneficiary's lawyer was evidence of the control the beneficiary had over the testator and the pressure that the beneficiary put on the testator to make the provisions he or she did in the will.

Example

Ethan constantly visits his uncle Jacob, an 88-year-old retired business tycoon, in the nursing home. During his visits, Ethan continuously urges Jacob to leave his vast business interests to him – to the detriment of Jacob's own children who don't visit as often as they should. Ethan, knowing that Jacob is lonely and depressed, threatens to stop visiting him as he is clearly ungrateful for Ethan's kindness and attention. Ethan finally arrives at the nursing home with his lawyer, who has never met Jacob before. Ethan remains present while Jacob instructs the lawyer to write a new will for him in which he purports to leave all his business interests to Ethan.

Ideally, an ethical lawyer should never agree to make a will or codicil in such circumstances, but in reality, it does happen. Therefore, it's always wise to get independent legal advice when you make a will or codicil.

Wills Made in Other Provinces

Generally speaking, wills made in one province are effective in all other provinces in Canada. However, when it comes to probate, in addition to filing the will for probate in the province in which the testator resided, the will may also need to be filed for probate in each province in which the testator held assets. This is particularly true in cases where the testator held valuable real estate in provinces outside his or her province of residence. Fortunately, if the assets located in a particular province are minimal in value, there may be a simplified means of 'probating' those assets without conducting a full-scale probate. Availing of these simplified procedures will save your estate considerable money and avoid delays in the long run.

If you require specific information regarding the probate of assets in other provinces, we recommend that you seek legal advice from a qualified and experienced lawyer.

Gifts and Beneficiaries

Gifting Your Assets

Before you start to make your will, you will need to make a list of all your assets & liabilities. This will give you an indication of what you have available to give to your beneficiaries. You can use the Will Writing Worksheet at the back of this kit to help you prepare this list. Once the list is prepared, the next step will be to decide who you want to gift your assets to.

For the most part, you are generally free to gift your assets as you wish. However, there are some restrictions on this freedom. Specifically, the laws in each province give rights to the spouse, children and other dependents of a deceased person to make a specific claim against the deceased's estate irrespective of what has been allocated to them under the terms of the deceased's will or on intestacy. These rights are typically classified as "spousal rights" or "dependent's relief".

Spouses' Rights

The laws in many provinces provide that if you die leaving a spouse, he or she will be entitled to receive a specific minimum portion of your estate on your death irrespective of what you may have left him or her in your will or irrespective of the portion they are entitled to on intestacy. This portion is known as the spouse's right. The size of your spouse's share will depend on the specific family laws applicable in your province of residence.

In brief, a surviving spouse will have the option of choosing to take either their legal right share as set out under the family law legislation in his/her province of residence or whatever has been left to him/her under the deceased spouse's will or on intestacy. Normally, a spouse will only elect to take the legal right share if they have been left less than their minimum entitlement under the deceased spouse's will or on intestacy. The surviving spouse will be afforded a specific period of time within which to make an election. The time frames for making an election in each province are set out in the table below. If the surviving spouse has not elected to take the legal right share before the expiry of the prescribed time frame, he/she will be obliged to accept whatever has been left to him/her under the deceased spouse's will or on intestacy.

Spousal Rights by Province			
Province	Definition of Spouse	Election Period	Priority of Spousal Claim Over Dependent's Relief Claim
Alberta	Legally married spouses only, and adult interdependent partners of not less than three years or someone who cohabited in a relationship of some permanence with the deceased if there is a child of the relationship, but excludes spouses that are separated.	Within six months of the issue of the grant of probate or letters of administration.	Spousal claim takes priority.
Manitoba	Legally married spouses and common law partners who have either registered under the Vital Statistics Act or been in a conjugal relationship for at least three years.	Unless extended by the court, within six months of the issue of the grant of probate or letters of administration.	Spousal claim takes priority.
New Brunswick	Legally married spouses only.	Unless extended by the court, within four months of the deceased spouse's death.	Spousal claim takes priority.
Newfoundland & Labrador	Legally married spouses only.	Unless extended by the court, within one year of the deceased spouse's death.	Not stated.

Northwest Territories & Nunavut	Legally married spouses and common law partners who have either (i) lived in a conjugal relationship for at least two years or (ii) lived in a form of permanent relationship with each other whereby the surviving spouse is the natural or adoptive parent of a child with the deceased spouse.	Within six months of the issue of the grant of probate or letters of administration.	Spousal claim takes priority.
Nova Scotia	Legally married spouses and common law partners who have registered under the Vital Statistics Act.	Unless extended by the court, within six months of the issue of the grant of probate or letters of administration.	Not stated.
Ontario	Legally married spouses only.	Within six months of the deceased spouse's death.	Spousal claim takes priority save where the claim is made by a child of the deceased.
Quebec	Legally married spouses and partners who have registered a civil union (whether same or opposite sex relationship).	None specified.	Spousal claim takes priority
Saskatchewan	Legally married spouses and common law partners who have been in a relationship for at least two years.	Within six months of the issue of the grant of probate or letters of administration.	Spousal claim takes priority.

Spousal claims are not permitted in British Columbia, Prince Edward Island or Yukon. However, in the cases of Prince Edward Island and Yukon, if a claim had been instituted before the deceased spouse's death for a distribution of the marital assets on the foot of a marital breakdown, that claim may be continued after the spouse's death.

Similarly, in Alberta, the spousal claim is only permitted in circumstances where there has been a marital breakdown prior to the deceased spouse's death and there has been no formal division of the marital assets arising from that breakdown. As mentioned above, the surviving spouse will have a period of six months from the date of issue of the grant of probate or letters of administration to take that claim.

Dependants' Relief

Each province in Canada has legislation which allows dependants of a deceased person to apply for support from the deceased's estate where they believe that the distribution of the deceased's estate, under the terms of the deceased's will or in some cases on intestacy, failed to make adequate provision for them. In each of British Columbia and Nova Scotia, dependent's relief will not apply in cases of intestacy – but still apply in relation to distributions under a will.

While the definition of a 'dependent' varies from province to province, it is generally taken to include spouses (including common law and same sex spouses), children (including legitimate and illegitimate children of the deceased) and, in certain cases, other people who were financially dependent on the deceased at the time of the deceased's death.

It's worth pointing out that, in certain cases, it's not sufficient to simply fall within a class of dependents, a person must have actually been financially dependent on the deceased before they can become entitled to make a claim.

Similar to the position with spousal rights above, in order for a dependent to make a claim against the deceased's estate, he or she must institute the relevant claim within a specific period of time. The timelines for making a claim in each province are set out in the table below.

Where a claim for dependent's relief is made and the court is of the opinion that the person has failed in his or her moral duty to make adequate provision for the proper support of his or her dependents, the court may order that such provision shall be made for the dependent out of the deceased's estate in such manner as the court sees fit. In assessing claims, a court will typically consider the following issues:-

- the moral duties of the deceased towards the dependent;

- any reasons provided by the testator (where a will was made) for not providing further for a particular dependent;

- the financial needs and position of the dependent – although this is not necessarily a criterion for a successful claim; and

- how the assets of the deceased's estate might have been distributed on a divorce (which could include support for both spouse and children).

Where the court orders a redistribution of a deceased person's estate, this could have a significant impact on some of the other gifts made under the deceased's will.

Dependent Rights by Province		
Province	Definition of Dependent	Election Period
Alberta	• Legal spouse; • Adult interdependent partner; • Child under the age of 18 years; and • Child over the age of 18 who is suffering from a mental or physical disability which prevents him or her from earning a livelihood.	Within six months of the issue of the grant of probate or letters of administration.
British Columbia	• Legally married spouses and common law partners (of same or opposite sex) who have been in a marital like relationship for at least two years; and • Children including legitimate, illegitimate and adopted children. Stepchildren are excluded unless adopted.	Within six months of the issue of the grant of probate. Does not apply on intestacy.
Manitoba	• Legal spouse; • Divorced spouse in receipt of maintenance; • Common law partner; • Child under the age of 18 years; • Child over the age of 18 who is suffering from a mental or physical disability which prevents him or her from earning a livelihood; and • Child, grandchild, sibling, parent or grandparent who was financially dependent on the deceased at the time of the deceased's death.	Within six months of the issue of the grant of probate or letters of administration.

New Brunswick	• Legal spouse; • Common law partner; • Child under the age of 19 years; and • Parent who previously supported the deceased and who was financially dependent on the deceased at the time of the deceased's death.	Within four months of the deceased's death.
Newfoundland & Labrador	• Legal spouse; and • Child under the age of 19 years.	Within six months of the issue of the grant of probate or letters of administration.
Northwest Territories & Nunavut	• Legal spouse; • Child under the age of 19 years; • Child over the age of 19 who is suffering from a mental or physical disability which prevents him or her from earning a livelihood; and • A person who cohabited with the deceased for at least a year immediately prior to the deceased's death and who was financially dependent on the deceased; • A person who cohabited with the deceased and with whom the deceased had a child; and • A person who resided with the deceased, was a foster parent of the deceased's children and who was financially dependent on the children.	Within six months of the issue of the grant of probate or letters of administration.
Nova Scotia	• Legal spouse; • Registered domestic partner (registered under the Vital Statistics Act); and • Child (whether an adult or not).	Within six months of the issue of the grant of probate. Does not apply on intestacy.

Ontario	• Legal spouse; • Ex-spouse; • A common law partner who cohabited with the deceased for at least three years immediately prior to the deceased's death or was in a relationship of some permanence with the deceased if, together with the deceased, they were the natural or adoptive parents of a child; and • Child, grandchild, sibling, parent or grandparent provided that, at the time of the deceased's death, the deceased was legally obliged to provide support for such person.	Within six months of the issue of the grant of probate or letters of administration.
Prince Edward Island	• Legal spouse; • Ex-spouse; • A common law partner (of the opposite sex) who cohabited with the deceased for at least three years immediately prior to the deceased's death and was financially dependent on the deceased; • Child under the age of 18 years; • Child over the age of 18 who is suffering from a mental or physical disability which prevents him or her from earning a livelihood; and • Child, grandchild, parent, grandparent or divorced spouse of the deceased who resided with the deceased for at least three years immediately prior to the deceased's death and was financially dependent on the deceased.	Within six months of the issue of the grant of probate or letters of administration.
Quebec	• Legal spouse; • Ex-spouse; • Child; and • Parent	Within four months of the deceased's death.

| Saskatchewan | • Legal spouse;

• A common law partner who cohabited with the deceased for at least two years immediately prior to the deceased's death or was in a relationship of some permanence with the deceased if, together with the deceased, they were the parents of a child;

• Child under the age of 18 years; and

• Child over the age of 18 who is either suffering from a mental or physical disability which prevents him or her from earning a livelihood, or by reason of necessity should be entitled to a larger share of the deceased's estate. | Within six months of the issue of the grant of probate or letters of administration. |

In Quebec, the dependent's relief is called "the survival of the obligation to provide support" while the dependent is also commonly referred to as the "creditor of support". In addition, the law in Quebec places specific limitations on the amounts that a dependent can claim from a deceased's estate.

Recommendation

If you have any concerns relating to the entitlements of your spouse or dependents to a share in your estate, we recommend that you speak to a lawyer.

Types of Gifts

A gift can generally be defined as a voluntary transfer of property from one person to another made gratuitously, without any consideration or compensation. Under your will, you can leave gifts of either financial or personal value to your family and friends. These gifts can come in the form of gifts of a specific item, gifts of cash or gifts of the residuary of your estate. Each of these forms of gift is explained below.

Specific Item Gifts

A specific item gift (also known as a legacy or bequest) is a gift of a specific item to a named beneficiary. Gifts of this type typically include items such as, for example, a car, a piece of jewelry, stocks, bonds, land, houses and so on. When you are inserting details of a specific item gift in your will, it is important to ensure that you clearly identify and describe the item that you wish to gift. So, for example, where you are gifting a car, you should describe the make, model and colour of the car rather than simply referring to "my car". This reduces the risk of confusion over what you intended in your will – especially if you have more than one car at the time of your death. When writing a provision for a gift, a good question to ask yourself is whether a stranger reading your will would easily understand exactly what you wanted to gift. If not, you need to re-write that clause.

Cash Gifts

A cash gift (also known as monetary or pecuniary legacy) is a gift of a specific amount of money to a named beneficiary. Just as with specific items gifts, when making a cash gift you need to clearly specify the amount that you are gifting (including the currency) and the person to whom you wish to make the gift to. In addition, when making a cash gift, it is important that you consider the financial implications on the overall estate. Remember, you may need to ensure that sufficient funds are readily available to meet the needs of your dependents or to discharge any taxes or expenses (including funeral expenses) which might be payable following your death. So be careful not to exhaust your cash too quickly – otherwise other assets may need to be sold to raise funds to discharge these obligations.

Gift of the Residuary Estate

This is simply a gift of the residue or remainder of an estate to one or more named beneficiaries. The residue of an estate (or residuary estate, as it's often called) is the remainder of a deceased person's estate after the payment of all debts, funeral and testamentary expenses and after all specific item and cash gifts have been made. The residuary also includes property that is the subject of a failed gift. A gift fails in circumstances where the beneficiary has died before becoming entitled to the gift or refuses to accept the gift. The person entitled to receive a gift of the residuary estate under a will is called the residuary beneficiary or, if there is more than one beneficiary, the residuary beneficiaries.

What Assets Can I Gift Under My Will?

When it comes to making your will, it's important to understand that only assets which form part of your estate can be gifted in your will. In general terms, your estate comprises of all the assets that you own outright such as your real estate, property, cash, investments, insurance policies, valuables, cars, jewelry and so on.

There is, however, a number of assets which fall outside of your estate. Knowing what these assets are is important for two very specific reasons. Firstly, and most obviously, by knowing what assets you cannot gift under your will, you can easily identify those assets which you can gift. Secondly, by knowing the types of assets which fall outside of your estate, you can plan your estate in a manner that allows for some of your assets to pass to your proposed beneficiaries without having them tied up in the probate process. This is because only those assets which pass under your will need to go through probate. This is important because you can construct your estate in a way that allows your estate to pass to your beneficiaries quite quickly and in a manner which reduces probate fees.

The most common forms of assets which don't pass under your estate and don't go through probate include the following:-

(i)   joint bank accounts;

(ii)   insurance policies;

(iii)   RRSPs, RRIFs, LIRA and pensions;

(iv)   jointly owned property; and

(v)   property in a revocable living trust.

Joint Bank Accounts

An easy way to avoid probate is by having joint bank accounts. Where an account is held in the name of two or more persons and is designated with the right of survivorship, then when one of the account holders dies, the surviving account holders will automatically acquire the deceased account holder's interest in the account. Whoever is the last surviving joint owner will ultimately own the proceeds of the account outright.

Where a transfer occurs on survivorship, there is no need for probate. The surviving account holder(s) will simply need to provide a copy of the deceased account holder's death certificate to the bank and the bank can then remove that person's name from the account.

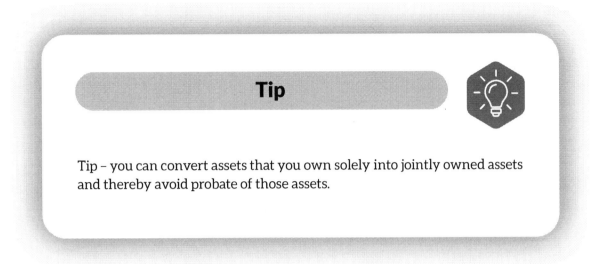

Tip

Tip – you can convert assets that you own solely into jointly owned assets and thereby avoid probate of those assets.

Life Insurance Proceeds

A life policy is another example of a simple means by which you can avoid probate. Where you designate a named beneficiary under your life insurance policy, the proceeds of the policy which are payable on your death will pass directly to the named beneficiary without the need to go through probate. However, if your estate is named as the main beneficiary (which is unusual) or if no beneficiaries have been named or if the named beneficiaries have died, the proceeds will need to pass to your estate and go through probate.

RRSPs, RRIFs, LIRAs and Pensions

Similar to the position with insurance policies, it's possible to designate beneficiaries for a number of other assets. These assets include things line RRSPs, RRIFs, LIRAs and pensions. In the same way as with insurance, when you die, the assets will be passed to the named beneficiaries without the need for probate.

Joint Ownership of Property

Whether or not the property that you own at the time of your death will need to be probated depends on how the title to that property is held. Typically, property can be held in two different ways namely (i) joint tenancy (survivorship) and (ii) tenancy in common.

(i) Joint tenancy

We've already touched on the concept of joint tenancy in relation to bank accounts above. The same principle applies to real estate. Where a property is held under a joint tenancy, each of the property owners has an undivided percentage interest in the entire property. To illustrate this, an example is often useful. So, let's, for example, take a case where four people own a property equally under a joint tenancy arrangement. Each of the four owners has an entitlement to a 25% interest in the entire or whole of the property.

Where one of the joint tenants dies, their share passes to the remaining joint tenants. Taking our example again, where one of the four property owners die, their share passes to each of the other three survivors automatically and each of the survivors then becomes entitled to an approximate 33.33% (or 1/3) interest in the property.

The key point to take from the above is that the share passes from the deceased joint owner to the remaining joint owners without the need for probate. It follows that probate can either be reduced or even eliminated by converting solely owned assets into jointly owned assets – held under a joint tenancy. This type of ownership permits the jointly owned assets to simply pass directly to the surviving joint owners on the death of one of the owners – no need for probate.

(ii) Tenancy in common

A tenancy in common is one of the most common forms of property ownership in Canada. A tenancy in common is created where two or more people purchase a property together as 'tenants in common'. As tenants in common, each of the parties own a separate and distinguishable part of the property. To take the example of our 4 property owners above, if the arrangement was a tenancy in common, each of them would own 25% of the property in their own right and would be free to sell that 25% to any person at any time and/or to dispose of their 25% interest under their will. The right of survivorship does not apply here.

Revocable Living Trust

An additional way to avoid probate is to establish and fund a revocable living trust. This type of trust is established under a written trust agreement. In essence, under the terms of the trust agreement, the creator of the trust (known as a grantor) will transfer ownership of certain of his assets into the trust. The trustee of the trust (which is also actually the grantor) will hold and manage the assets on behalf of the trust. The trustee can manage, invest, and spend the trust property as he or she sees fit for the benefit of the grantor and for the benefit of the ultimate beneficiaries of the trust.

Because the grantor will not own any property in his or her individual name after the assets have been transferred into the name of the trust, the assets will not need to be probated. When the grantor dies, the person nominated as the 'successor trustee' under the terms of the trust agreement will step into the grantor's shoes and will distribute the proceeds of the trust to the named beneficiaries in accordance with the terms of the trust agreement.

Recommendation

If you require further information on assets that do not go through probate, speak to a solicitor or view one of EstateBee other publications.

Types of Beneficiaries

A beneficiary is a person, organization or other entity that will inherit part of your assets or estate under your will. There are three main types of beneficiaries under a will. These include a specific gift beneficiary, an alternate beneficiary and a residuary beneficiary.

Specific Gift Beneficiary

A specific gift beneficiary is a person or organization named in your will to receive a cash gift or a specific item gift as defined above. Specific gifts are generally the first gifts distributed under a will. Any assets that are not specifically distributed under your will shall form part of the residuary estate (assuming that you have a catch all residuary clause – see below) and will usually be given (unless there are taxes or other expenses to be discharged) to the person or persons named as residuary beneficiary or beneficiaries, as the case may be.

Alternate Beneficiary

When naming beneficiaries to receive gifts under your will, it can be prudent (but is not obligatory) to prepare for the possibility that one or more of these beneficiaries will be unable (whether due to death or otherwise) or unwilling (for whatever reason) to accept the gifts made to them. To this end, it can be helpful to nominate alternate beneficiaries to receive the gift if the primary beneficiary is unable or unwilling to accept it. An alternate beneficiary is a person who becomes legally entitled to inherit a gift if the first named beneficiary is unable or unwilling to accept it. If no alternate beneficiary is named for the gift, the gift will form part of the residuary estate and go to the residuary beneficiary.

You can name more than one person as an alternate beneficiary. For example, you can appoint a second alternate beneficiary to receive a gift where the first alternate beneficiary is unable or unwilling to accept it. However, when doing this it is important that you fully consider the order in which the alternate beneficiaries become entitled to share the property and ensure that this order is correct.

Residuary Beneficiary

A residuary beneficiary is the person(s) or organization(s) named to receive the residue of your estate; they get what's left when all of the specific item gifts and cash gifts have been made and all debts and taxes have been paid.

Who May Not Be a Beneficiary?

While you are generally free to make gifts to anyone you choose, the law does place some restrictions on the people who can receive gifts from you under your will. In particular, the following persons or organizations will be precluded from receiving gifts from you under your will:

- a lawyer who is involved in drafting your will or in providing advice to you in connection with your will;
- a person who has witnessed the signing of your will;
- a person who unlawfully caused your death; and
- a company or unincorporated association that is not permitted to hold property under the terms of its constitutional documents.

Gifts to Charities

When it comes to making a will, many of us want to make a gift to our favourite charity. Doing this is relatively straightforward. All you need to do is identify the gift you wish to make and the charity that will receive the gift. You can gift money, specific items or nominate the charity as a beneficiary of the residuary of your estate – the choice is yours. However, if you choose to make a gift to a charity it's important to ensure that you provide clear details of the charity to be benefited. In this respect, it's useful to identity the charity by reference to its correct legal name (as it may differ from the 'trading name' commonly used by the charity) as well as its charity registration number. You can usually get these details from the charity's website.

Imposing Conditions on the Receipt of Gifts

In making a gift under your will, you may wish to provide that the beneficiary will only be entitled to receive that gift if certain conditions are satisfied. While this is perfectly acceptable, you do need to take extreme care when adding conditions. In fact, it's best to consult a lawyer when you are doing so.

There are two basic types of conditions that can be imposed on a beneficiary - conditions precedent and conditions subsequent.

A condition precedent is a requirement that must be met before the beneficiary is entitled to receive a gift. For example, you may specify that *"I give the sum of $5,000 to my nephew Ethan Smith if he has obtained a college degree in engineering before 31 December 2030. If my nephew Ethan Smith has not obtained the college degree as aforesaid, then I give the sum of $5,000 to my niece Emma Smith instead"*. The imposition of such a condition does not pose too many difficulties for the executor or trustee as it will be easy to determine whether the beneficiary has met the requirement or not....of course they may have to wait a while to find out. If the beneficiary fails to meet the requirements, then the proceeds being held by the executor or trustee to make this gift will be given to the alternate beneficiary or, where none is named, to the persons entitled to the residuary interest in the estate (i.e., the residuary beneficiaries).

A condition subsequent, on the other hand, is a requirement that must be met after the beneficiary receives the gift. These types of conditions cause a lot more problems than conditions precedent because often the gift is received on the condition that the beneficiary fulfils an obligation or a specific event occurs. Problems arise where the obligation is not fulfilled or the event never occurs.

If we took our example above and modified the condition such that it became a condition subsequent, it would read something like this *"I give the sum of $5,000 to my nephew Ethan Smith on the conditions that he uses this money to obtain a college degree in engineering before 31 December 2030. If my nephew Ethan Smith has not obtained the college degree as aforesaid, then I give the sum of $5,000 to my niece Emma Smith instead"*. In this instance, Ethan has received the gift before he has satisfied the condition. This of course can be problematic. What happens if Ethan fails to satisfy the condition within the required time frame? Well, Emma will need to try and recover the $5,000 from Ethan. This may be easier said than done of course.

While conditions being placed on the receipt of a gift are generally valid, there are some conditions that courts will refuse to enforce. Typically, these are conditions that are void for uncertainty (i.e., they are unclear) or void on the grounds of public policy. Conditions void on the grounds of public policy would, for example, include requirements that the beneficiary marry or refrain from marrying someone, divorce or refrain from divorcing someone, change religion or even murder someone. Conditions void for uncertainty are void simply because they are unclear and their performance cannot therefore be strictly observed.

Recommendation

We do not recommend that you include conditional gifts in your will without first speaking to a lawyer.

Releasing Someone from a Debt

Under your will you may release or "forgive" a debt owed to you by another person, incorporated body, or unincorporated association. This will legally release that person or entity from the debt on your death. If you do not forgive the debt, your executor will be entitled to institute legal proceedings on behalf of your estate in order to recover the monies from the debtor in question.

Failed Gifts

If you decide to gift a specific item to a beneficiary in your will and you subsequently dispose of that item before your death then, upon your death, the gift will fail because it cannot be completed. Where the gift fails, the intended beneficiary will not be entitled to receive a substitute gift under your will unless you have expressly provided for this in your will.

Additionally, if you gift a specific item or a particular amount of money to a named person and that person predeceases you then, unless an alternate beneficiary is entitled to receive that gift under the terms of your will, the gift reverts to form part of your residuary estate. An exception to this general principal arises under the 'per stirpes' rule mentioned above which provides that where a person makes a gift to their child and that child predeceases the parent, the gift will pass to the deceased child's estate. Depending on whether the child made a will or died intestate, the gift will be distributed to the deceased's child's beneficiaries/heirs.

An exception to the above rules arises in the case of gifts to charity and particularly gifts of the residuary estate to charity. Where a gift to a charity fails (either because the charity cannot be identified or because it has ceased to exist) and the court is satisfied that the testator intended to make a charitable gift, it can invoke the doctrine of Cy-près. This doctrine allows the court to make a substitute gift to charity in place of the failed gift where it believes that the donor genuinely wished to make a charitable gift.

Matters Affecting the Distribution of Your Assets

Before you make any decisions on how you wish to distribute your assets, it's useful to be aware of a number of specific events that can have an impact on how your assets are ultimately distributed. These events include the following: -

- simultaneous death;
- abatement of assets; and
- disclaimed inheritances.

We'll consider each of these further below.

Simultaneous Death

It is common in wills to insert what is known as a 'common disaster' or 'simultaneous death' provision. These types of provisions usually provide that in order for your beneficiary to receive a gift under your will, they must survive you for a period of say 30 to 60 days before they can inherit. This is aimed at the situation where, for example, you might die in an accident in which one or more of your named beneficiaries (particularly your spouse) are also fatally injured. If that beneficiary survives you, and there is no required survival period, he or she would be entitled to receive the gift immediately on your death. If that beneficiary then dies shortly after you, the beneficiary's heirs would in turn be entitled to receive the gift on probate of the first deceased beneficiary's estate. The provision is therefore designed to avoid multiple probates/administrations and taxes on the same assets where one or more of your beneficiaries die of injuries a few hours (or days) after you.

This common disaster provision is most commonly used between spouses and typically provides for the transfer of the estate to the surviving spouse but only if he or she survives the deceased spouse for a specified period of time following the death of the deceased spouse. If the 'surviving spouse' does not survive the 'deceased spouse' for the requisite time frame, the gift will pass to any alternate beneficiary named under the will to receive that gift or, where none is named, to the residuary beneficiaries.

Abatement of Assets

When the residuary of an estate is insufficient to pay the debts and taxes owing by an estate, it will become necessary to apply other assets of the estate to meet these payments. The process by which these assets are applied to pay the debts of the estate is known as abatement. When assets are abated, they are sold (if not already in cash form) to raise cash to discharge the debts of the estate. Generally, the first assets of an estate which are abated are legacies (i.e., the cash gifts). For example, if the estate has $50,000 in the bank account to cover cash gifts to the deceased's friends, and debts are still owing by the estate after the residuary estate has been dissipated, this money may be used to discharge these debts. Any of the $50,000 remaining after payment of the debts will be distributed pro rata to the relevant beneficiaries. However, if the funds are insufficient to pay off all of the debts, then the executor can begin to sell the items left as specific item gifts (i.e., antiques, jewelry, property, etc.) in order to raise the required funds.

As you will have gathered, the net result following the abatement process is that people who have been left gifts under your will may not receive anything if the estate has high levels of debt. As such, in making your will, you need to carefully consider the debt levels of your estate and even consider designating in your will the assets that you would like sold to meet those debts if there are insufficient reserves in the residuary estate to meet the payments.

Disclaimed Inheritances

A beneficiary can renounce or disclaim their entitlement to receive a gift under a will. This may be done for several reasons - because it's unwanted, carries heavy liabilities (property maintenance, for example), tax reasons, or because the intended beneficiary simply wants to pass the gift to another beneficiary. If an alternate beneficiary has been named in your will to receive that gift, he or she will then become entitled to it. If no alternate beneficiary is named, the gift will be passed to the beneficiary or beneficiaries entitled to the residue of the estate.

What if You Own Property Outside Canada?

As more and more people now own foreign properties it has become increasingly important to take account of these foreign assets in the preparation of wills. Of more importance, however, is the necessity to ensure that you do not inadvertently revoke an existing will when making a local or foreign will. This brief section explains how this could happen.

Generally, your foreign property is subject to the succession laws of the country in which the property is located. As such, it becomes necessary to execute a will dealing with your property in that country in order to record your wishes in relation to the foreign property. To prevent any new Canadian will revoking a foreign will relating only to property located in a foreign country, it is necessary to insert a clause in your Canadian will to the effect that it does not relate to any property held outside of Canada. A similar clause should be inserted into any foreign wills that you make so that they don't revoke any wills you have made in Canada.

As there are various estate taxation systems in existence in other countries, it is highly advisable to seek the advice of a national lawyer in the country or jurisdiction in which your foreign assets are held.

Resource

If you happen to own any assets (including real property, insurance or even stocks or shares) that are situated outside Canada and would like to make a will in respect of those assets please feel free to visit our website, **www.estate-bee.com** or any of our other EstateBee websites for further assistance.

A Special Request – Please Leave a Review on Amazon

Thank you for purchasing this Last Will & Testament Kit.

Your positive book review could really help us and help other customers make informed decisions when purchasing self-help kits like this one.

This link will take you to the Amazon.co.uk review page for this book. We would be very grateful if you could please leave a positive 5 Star Review.

Estate-bee.com/review30

Children, Guardians and Property Management

What is a Guardian?

A guardian is the person responsible for a child's (or other dependent or incapacitated person's) physical care, education, health and welfare; as well as for making decisions about the child's faith-related matters.

Normally, if you are married and have a child you and your spouse are the primary legal guardians of your minor children, including any children that you may have adopted together. If you pass away, then your surviving spouse (or the children's surviving parent) becomes the sole guardian of these children. However, if your surviving spouse also passes away, and neither of you have made any provisions for the appointment of a guardian, then the children could become the responsibility of the Public Trustee and the public welfare services. Where this happens, there is a real risk that your children could end up being cared for by people that you would never have wished to raise them.

If you have children, it is therefore vital to plan ahead and ensure that they will be properly cared for in the event that neither you nor your spouse (or the children's surviving parent) are around to do so. In this respect, you should give careful thought and consideration to naming a guardian and an alternate guardian in your will to take care of your children following your passing.

Sole and Joint Guardians

You have the option of appointing one or more guardians to care for your children. If you appoint one guardian, he or she will be known as a "sole guardian" and will be solely responsible for the welfare of your children and for making all decisions (including financial) on their behalf. Alternatively, you can also nominate two or more people to serve as joint guardians to the children. However, with joint guardians, each of them must reach agreement in relation to decisions regarding the children in their care, before any decision can be implemented. It is for this reason that joint guardians are usually only nominated where they are married to each other or live together, as well as where they each have an important relationship to the children (uncles or aunts, for example).

If you are considering appointing a married couple as joint guardians of your children, be sure to carefully consider the status of the couple's relationship and whether you would want both spouses to serve as guardians if they were ever separated or divorced. In such instances, it may be preferable to simply appoint one spouse as guardian at the very outset. The choice, however, is yours.

Alternate Guardians

When appointing a guardian, it is generally recommended that you also appoint an alternate guardian (or several alternates, hierarchically) who will serve if, for any reason, your first named guardian (known as your 'primary guardian') is unable or unwilling to serve when the time comes. If your first-choice guardian cannot serve and you fail to name an alternate guardian in your will, it will then fall for the court to step in and determine who will act as guardian to your children. As alluded to above, the court's appointee may not be someone that you would have approved of had you been given the opportunity to do so.

Who Can Be a Guardian?

The short answer is that anyone can be a guardian provided that they are agreeable to acting as a guardian to your children and are themselves an adult.

What to Consider When Choosing a Guardian for Your Children

As you will be leaving the responsibility of caring for your children to another person, the decision as to whom you should appoint as a guardian to your children is an extremely important one; and one that should not be made lightly. You will need to take many factors into consideration. Ultimately, however, you should choose the person you believe will offer the best care and support to your children. Often this will be a close relative or family friend. However, before actually appointing them as guardian under your will, it is very important that you check with your proposed nominee to ensure that he or she is willing to accept such a responsible and onerous role. There is no point in nominating someone if you think they will refuse to accept the role when the time comes.

Recommendation

Discuss your choice with the people you have selected as guardians and make sure they are willing to accept the responsibility should it become necessary.

There are many things that you will need to take into account when considering whether a person would be a good guardian to your children. In particular, you should ask yourself the following questions regarding the proposed nominee:

- is the person you are considering willing to accept the long-term responsibility of being a guardian to your children?

- is the person responsible and up to the task of raising your children?

- is the person old enough (at least over 18 years) to be a guardian?

- where does the person reside?

- would your children be uprooted and moved away from their friends and family members if they went to live with this guardian? Would that be in their best interests?

- if you have more than one child, do you want your children to remain together? If you do then be sure to name the same guardian for all your children.

- what is this person's home situation? For example, does he or she have a house or a one-bed apartment? Is the potential guardian in a stable relationship?

- will the potential guardian be able to provide your children with a stable positive environment and home life?

- will your children still have easy access to their other relatives – such as grandparents?

- what are the person's religious and moral beliefs?

- does the person have any medical conditions or other issues that would prevent them from being a suitable guardian?

● if you cannot make sufficient financial provision for your children's long-term care, will this person be able to afford to care for your children?

These are all very important and relative questions, but only the tip of the iceberg. There will no doubt be many other things that will influence your decision. So, take your time to think things through thoroughly.

Once you have selected someone to act as a guardian to your children, it is important to discuss the potential appointment with him or her (or them) in detail. While most people are flattered, you will find that some are unable or unwilling to accept the responsibility. Be wary also of people agreeing to accept the role insincerely in the expectation that they will never be called upon to act. This is another very good reason to appoint an alternate guardian - just in case the primary guardian is unable or unwilling to assume the role when the time comes.

Management of Children's Property

While the appointment of a guardian to care for and to raise your child is important, it is equally important to consider who will manage the money and property your child inherits from you; and indeed, from anyone else. This is because children who have not yet reached the age of majority lack sufficient legal capacity to receive and manage inherited property. While this lack of capacity is often not an issue for most minors, it is problematic where they inherit significant or valuable assets. In such cases, it will be necessary to appoint an adult called a 'trustee' or 'property guardian' to receive and manage the property on behalf of the minor.

If you don't make arrangements to provide for the future management of your children's property, the court will do it for you by appointing a 'property guardian' of its choosing to manage the inheritances. Like the situation with normal guardians, a court will often appoint the surviving parent, but this is not always the case. A third party or court appointed guardian can be appointed to deal with the property and, in such cases, that property guardian will have complete control over your children's inheritance. As such, it is important that you deal with this appointment in your will or in another legal agreement.

Fortunately, it is relatively easy and straightforward to avoid the uncertainties and hassles of a court-appointed guardianship. You can choose someone now to manage any property that your minor or young adult children may someday inherit from you. While there are many ways that you can structure this arrangement, here are three of the simplest and most common methods.

Appointment of a property guardian

A property guardian is a person you appoint to be responsible for managing the property you leave to your children plus any other property that your children might receive. A property guardian is bound to manage the property in your children's best interests, using it to pay for normal living expenses, as well as health and educational needs.

If you name a property guardian for your children in your will, when the time comes, the court will (in the absence of strong reasons to do otherwise) formally appoint your selected person as property guardian to your children.

While a property guardian is appointed under the terms of your will, the scope of his or her management authority extends beyond the management of property left to your children under your will. In fact, it extends to include any property later received by your children where there are no pre-existing arrangements for management of that property (such as under a trust). As such, should your children receive an inheritance from a long lost relative, their property guardian is authorized to manage that property in the absence of your relative having provided for a specific means of management.

Remember, a property guardian is different to a personal guardian; the latter guardian is responsible for the care, health, welfare and education of the child. A property guardian is only responsible for managing the child's property – although he or she can apply the managed property for the benefit of the child's care, health, welfare or education. Do not make the mistake of appointing only a property guardian and thinking that he or she will also be responsible for the day-to-day care of the child.

Individual child trusts

A child's trust is valid in all provinces and can be created under the terms of a will (such trusts are often called testamentary trust) or a living trust (such trusts are known as child sub-trusts).

A trust is a fiduciary arrangement whereby a person is appointed to become the legal owner of trust property, which they will hold for the benefit of another person. A child trust is a trust created for the benefit of a child. You can create a separate child trust for each of your children (if you wish) and for any other minor who stands to inherit under the terms of your will or living trust.

In your will or living trust document, you can name a trustee (usually a trusted relative or friend) who will manage the inheritance that a child will receive (as a beneficiary of that trust) until that child reaches an age specified by you. If the child in question has reached that age at the time of your death, and is past the age of majority for their province, the trust never actually comes into existence and the property is instead transferred directly to them upon your death.

However, where your child is under the age specified in your will or trust document, the inheritance will be transferred to a separate trust fund and will be managed by the nominated trustee in accordance with provisions set out in your will or trust document. The trustee will continue to manage the trust property until the child in question has reached the age specified in your will or trust document. At that time, the remainder of the trust property will be transferred to the now adult beneficiary and the trust will be terminated.

During the course of the trust, the trustee will have broad discretion over the management and distribution of the trust property. If the trustee deems it appropriate, he or she can release monies to or make payments on behalf of the child to cover matters ranging from education, medical and general maintenance.

While court supervision is generally not required with these types of trusts, serving as a trustee can be very onerous. For example, a trustee is required to file annual income tax returns for the child trust with the Canada Revenue Agency. Also, because the powers of trustees of a child's trust are set out in the will or trust document itself, it will be necessary for the trustee to produce copies of the relevant document every time he or she has to deal with a financial institution on behalf the minor child.

Family trusts

A family trust is a good tool to use with younger children. Family trusts are a legal device that allows you to place monies in trust to benefit two or more of your minor children. Family trusts, however, are somewhat unique in that trust assets are made available to whichever child needs them most rather than being divided equally for the benefit of each child. With a family trust, your trustee has discretion to apportion the trust funds between the children as he or she sees fit. So, for example, if one of your children wishes to go to college, your trustee can take a portion of the money from the trust to send that child to college. Similarly, should one of your children require an expensive medical treatment, monies can be released from the trust to cover the costs of the treatment.

A family trust will terminate when the youngest child reaches a specified age (known as the age of termination of the trust) which is usually 18 to 30 years of age. At that time, the trust fund is divided between the beneficiaries equally.

One of the principal drawbacks to using a family trust is that older children will not receive their share of the balance of the trust property until the youngest child reaches the designated age of termination of the trust. As such, they may well be into adulthood by the time they receive their shares of the inheritance.

Whom Should You Choose as a Trustee?

A trustee's duties can continue for a number of years and, in many cases, may require expertise in investing money, dealing with property, paying bills, filing accounts and managing money on behalf of the trust's underlying beneficiaries. As such, you will need to carefully consider your choice of proposed trustee. In many cases, people who establish a trust tend to choose a family member or close friend as trustee as they tend not to charge fees for carrying out the role. This is absolutely fine so long as the person is capable of handling the financial matters involved and has sufficient time to carry out the role – and of course is willing to do so...remember to check with them first.

Professional trustees, on the other hand, will charge annual management fees for providing trustee services. In some instances, these fees can be quite substantial. However, given the expertise that a professional trustee can bring to the table, it is important to at least consider engaging them where you have a large estate.

If you decide not to use a professional trustee and opt for a family member or friend instead, then the characteristics that you should look for in your nominee are honesty, intelligence, diligence and conscientiousness. Having these qualities, above all else, will at least go some way towards ensuring that you pick the right person for the job. Remember, that your trustee can always get investment advice if he or she feels it necessary or helpful!

Executors

Executors

An executor is the person named in a will to carry out the administration of the deceased's estate in accordance with the provisions of that will. If the deceased failed to make a valid will, or where there is a partial intestacy, the court will appoint a person known as an administrator to wind up the affairs of the deceased (or deal with those assets not dealt with under the will) in accordance with the intestacy laws.

Did You Know

In Quebec, the executor of a will is sometimes referred to as a 'liquidator of the succession'. The 'succession' is another name for the 'estate'.

When making a will, you are free to appoint anyone you wish to act as your executor provided they are an adult and of sound mind. In this regard, you can appoint a relative, a beneficiary under your will, a lawyer or even a bank or professional trustee - the choice is yours. It is also possible to appoint more than one person to act as your executor. Where more than one executor is appointed, these co-executors can act separately (each one with full authority to act on behalf of your estate) or they can be required under the terms of your will to act jointly in which case both executors (or all executors, if there are more than two) must agree to a course of action before taking that action.

Upon your death, your executor will have the legal responsibility and fiduciary duty to handle, safeguard and distribute your property in accordance with the terms of your will. In addition, your executor will also be responsible for procuring the payment of any debts or taxes owing by you or your estate at the date of your death. These debts and taxes, if any, will be paid from your estate (using the assets of the estate) before the distribution of the remainder of the estate's property to the beneficiaries named under your will.

Alternate Executors

When making your will, it's always a good idea to appoint one or more alternate executors. An alternate executor is someone who will perform the duties of the first named executor should they be unable or unwilling to do so (for whatever reason). If the alternate executor is required to act, he or she will be bound by the same legal responsibilities and fiduciary duties as the original executor.

Overview of Executors' Duties

An executor's duties will usually include locating, collecting, assessing and managing the estate's assets; arranging the discharge of debts and taxes owing by the estate; distributing cash gifts and specific item gifts in accordance with the terms of the deceased's will; and entering into appropriate contracts to effect the transfer of real property from the estate to the relevant beneficiary named under the testator's will. It is also the executor's duty to report the testator's death to insurance companies, banks, and other institutions that might owe money to or hold money on behalf of the estate.

Who Should Be Your Executor?

Choosing an executor is one of the most fundamental tasks associated with making a will. Getting the choice right can mean the difference between a smooth administration on one hand and a tardy administration with unexpected delays and costs on the other hand. It's therefore important to take your time and make the correct choice. Typically, the characteristics to look for in a good executor include good common sense, excellent organizational skills and integrity.

Of course, many people tend to choose their spouse, a sibling, an adult child or a good friend as their executor. Others choose professionals such as a lawyer, accountant or professional trustee. All are good choices provided that the person chosen is both competent and trustworthy.

Other things being equal, it will often pay to choose a family member or friend as executor for the simple reason that these people expect little (if any) compensation in return for their time, will respect your wishes, and are generally keen to process and finalize things as quickly as possible. However, keep in mind that the process can be quite administrative, and time is often of the essence. So, you should still ensure that you choose someone who is organizationally reliable and generally up to the task.

It is not enough, however, to simply appoint someone who has all the hallmarks of a good executor. You must actually appoint someone who is willing to take on the role as it is always open for a person to refuse to accept the role despite being nominated in a will. In fact, many often refuse to act as executors because they are either too busy to take on the task or feel daunted by the prospect of doing so.

If your chosen executor refuses the appointment, a court will appoint someone else to fulfil the role. Usually, this will be a relative, a beneficiary under your will or a creditor of your estate.

Once you have decided on who you would like to appoint as your executor, it's important that you actually discuss your choice with them before actually naming them in your will. You will need to explain to your proposed executor the nature of his or her role and that it may not be a straightforward and easy process. If, after explaining the role, your nominee is willing to take on the task, then you should be free to formally appoint them under your will.

A Special Request – Please Leave a Review on Amazon

Thank you for purchasing this Last Will & Testament Kit.

Your positive book review could really help us and help other customers make informed decisions when purchasing self-help kits like this one.

This link will take you to the Amazon.co.uk review page for this book. We would be very grateful if you could please leave a positive 5 Star Review.

Estate-bee.com/review30

A Brief Introduction to Tax

Introduction

The information below is provided as a brief overview of taxation in Canada. If you have any tax queries relating to the disposal or distribution of your estate, it is recommended that you speak to a qualified lawyer or tax advisor.

Overview of The Canadian Tax System

Until the 1970s, Canada operated both an estate tax and a gift tax system which was broadly similar to what is in operation in the U.S. today. These systems, in essence, placed a tax on the transfer of assets from one person to another where the value of those assets exceeded a specified amount. Where the value of the assets exceeded this amount, a tax was imposed on the excess. There were, as you might expect, various exemptions and reliefs available against these taxes.

These taxes were however phased out in 1971 when the government opted to use a 'capital gains' type system whereby people were only changed a transfer tax where the value of the asset in question had increased since the current owner acquired it. The result was that people were generally free to transfer assets during their lifetime or on death without triggering a charge to tax provided the asset had not increased in value. However, if there was any gain in the value of the asset a charge to tax arose.

Capital Gains Tax

For convenience, we will talk about capital gains tax in this section. However, the reality is that there is no separate tax on capital gains in Canada. Instead, capital gains are taxed based on the owner's marginal rate of income tax.

A capital gain normally occurs when the proceeds of a sale of capital property (such as a house or shares in a company) are more than the original cost (known as the 'base cost') of that asset plus its adjusted cost base. We will ignore the adjusted cost base for now and illustrate how a capital gain arises with the help of an example.

Example

Jacob bought a holiday home in 1985 for $150,000 (the 'base cost'). He sold the property in 2021 for the hefty price of $900,000. The capital gain on the property is the difference between the price Jacob paid for the property (base cost) and the price he received when selling it. In this case, the gain is $750,000. The gain then becomes subject to income tax at Jacob's marginal rate. We'll look at how the tax is calculated further below.

What is a Capital Loss?

A capital loss occurs when the proceeds (or deemed proceeds) of a disposition of a capital property are less than its adjusted base cost. Where this occurs, the loss can be offset against any gains that an individual might have arising from the ownership of other assets. However, only half of the capital loss can be used to offset a capital gain.

If your capital losses exceed your capital gains, you cannot generally set off the additional capital losses against your other income tax liabilities. However, there are some exceptions to this general rule which arise in relation to investments made in Canadian companies. For further information, you should speak to your tax advisor.

Calculating the Adjusted Base Cost

As mentioned above, the base cost of an asset is usually the cost price of the asset. However, there are situations in which this base cost can be adjusted. Specifically, where the owner of an asset, such as a house for example, makes any capital expenditure on that house he or she is entitled to add the amount of that capital expenditure onto the base cost of the house for calculating any related capital gains. Obviously, where the base cost is adjusted upwards the amount of the gain will be reduced and with it the amount of income tax paid on the gain.

Example

Jacob bought a holiday home in 1985 for $150,000 (the 'base cost'). During the time in which he owned the holiday home, he added a new kitchen for $25,000 and built an extension for $100,000. These additions of $125,000 can be added to the original base cost of $150,000 to give a new adjusted base cost of $275,000.

Jacob sold the property in 2021 for a price of $900,000. The capital gain on the property is the difference between the base cost (as adjusted) of the house and the price he received when selling it. In this case, given the adjusted base cost, the gain is $625,000. The gain again becomes subject to income tax at Jacob's marginal rate.

Deemed Disposal on Death

Under Section 70 of the Income Tax Act (Canada), a person is deemed to have disposed of all his property immediately prior to his/her death and received the proceeds of that sale. The effect of the deemed disposal is to crystallize any capital gains that are inherent in the disposed assets. These gains then become chargeable to tax at the individual's marginal rate of income tax.

Did You Know

A disposal occurs where a person transfers the beneficial interest in an asset to another person such as, for example, where a piece of real estate is sold to another person. A deemed disposal is a notional sale for the purpose of creating a charge to tax.

Example

JJacob bought a holiday home in 1985 for $150,000. When Jacob died in 2021, the market value of the property was $900,000. Under the Income Tax Act, Jacob is deemed to have sold the property for its fair market value immediately prior to his death and received the proceeds of that sale. He must now pay income tax on any capital gain in the property. As already mentioned, the capital gain on the property is the difference between the price Jacob paid for it and its current market value. In this case, the gain is $750,000. The gain then becomes subject to income tax at Jacob's marginal rate which could be up to 50% if he was paying tax at the higher rate. This would mean that a tax bill of approximately $375,000 would have to be paid by Jacob's estate.

We have ignored the adjusted base cost in this example for ease. However, it can still apply. We have also ignored a 50% discount which can apply to gains – which we discuss further below.

Calculating the Fair Market Value

To determine the capital gain applicable to a particular asset owned by a deceased owner, it will be necessary to determine the fair market value of that asset on the date of the deceased owner's death. There are several ways of doing this.

In the cases of publicly quoted stock, you can check out the price on the internet or simply contact a stockbroker who can give you the price. In the case of privately held companies, it will be necessary to have the deceased owner's share valued by an accountant. The precise value of the shares will be influenced by the rights attaching to the shares and the percentage holding that these shares represent in the company as a whole.

Real estate on the other hand will require a valuation from a licensed real estate valuer.

Amount of Income Tax Payable on a Capital Gain

Under current law, only 50% of the actual capital gain is subject to income tax. This means that if you make a gain of $100,000, you will only be charged to income tax on $50,000.

The exact rate at which an individual will pay income tax on a gain will vary from province to province and from individual to individual depending on their current income levels, provincial income tax laws and allowable expenditures and reliefs. You should check with your tax advisor to determine what level of tax your estate might need to pay on the deemed disposal of assets on your death. In most provinces, the maximum applicable income tax rate payable at the higher marginal rate is around 50%.

Gifts to Spouse

If you leave any of your capital assets (including RRSP's) to your spouse on your death, there will be no charge to capital gains tax on those assets on your death. This is because, for tax purposes, there is no deemed disposition of your assets in favor of your spouse. Instead, a charge to capital gains tax will arise when your spouse disposes of these assets during his/her lifetime or at the time of his/her death.

RRSP's and Life Insurance

If you have not gifted the proceeds of your RRSP to your spouse, income tax will be payable on these proceeds on your death. Life insurance proceeds, on the other hand, are exempt from capital gains tax.

Principal Residence Exemption

It's possible to avail of a capital gains tax relief on the disposal or deemed disposal of your principal residence. Your principal residence can include a house, condominium, cottage, mobile home, trailer, houseboat or share in a co-operative building that is ordinarily inhabited for some part of the year by you, your spouse/civil partner, your former spouse/civil partner, or your children. It can also include any land on which that residence is situated provided it is of a certain size. The size permitted is usually limited to half a hectare. However, this size may be extended where the excess land is required to provide access to and from public roads.

It is important to note that the above requirements only stipulate that you inhabit the property for part of the year. Therefore, it is possible to own more than one property and chose which one you designate as your principal residence. Of course, you still need to reside in the property habitually – if only for the summer or winter months.

Where you designate a property as your primary residence, and you have occupied that property as your sole residence since acquiring it, there will be no charge to capital gains tax on the deemed disposal of this property on your death. However, if the property has not always been your principal residence since acquiring it, relief from capital gains will be applied on a pro rata basis based on the following formula:

$$\frac{(\text{Number of years the home has been your principal residence} + 1)}{\text{Number of years home is owned}} \times \text{capital gain} = \text{taxable gain}$$

Note: The extra year that is added in the top line of the equation is to allow for the inclusion of both the old property and the new property as a principal residence in the year in which the family moved to the new property, even though only one of them can be designated as such for that year.

Did You Know

A taxpayer and spouse may only designate one principal residence between them for each tax year after 1981.

If you own more than one home for any period after 1981 and each home can qualify as a principal residence, then it is generally suggested that you designate the home with the greatest average annual increase in value as your principal residence for the maximum number of years possible. This will be the number of years of ownership minus one (due to the bonus year in the numerator of the formula).

Did You Know

For more information about this relief, you should speak to your tax advisor.

Gifts Made During Your Lifetime

There is no tax on cash gifts in Canada. This is because, in theory, all cash which is gifted has already been subjected to income tax before the donor made the gift. However, while cash can be gifted tax free, attention does need to be paid to the gifting of assets. Where assets are gifted from one person to another, they will be deemed to have been gifted at their fair market value. So, for example, if you decide to make a gift of the shares you bought in Apple for $1,000 to your favorite nephew, you will be deemed to have disposed of them at their fair market value. If the fair market value of these shares was $5,000 at the time you made the gift, you will be liable to income tax on the remaining $4,000 at your marginal rate.

Capital Gains Deduction

If you have made a capital gain on the disposal of certain assets, you may be eligible for the $446,109 lifetime capital gains deduction. This equates to half of the $892,218 lifetime capital gains exemption – remember you only include half the gain in your income tax returns. These rates are current as of 2021 and are indexed annually to match the official rate of inflation as published by Statistics Canada.

The exemption is cumulative, and you can claim any part of it at any time in your life if you dispose of a qualifying asset. You do not have to claim the entire exemption amount at once. For example, if you sold company shares, say, three years ago and claimed $200,000 of exemption, you still have $692,218 available to claim.

Did You Know

A capital deduction is an amount that you can claim to reduce the amount of any capital gain that you have made on the disposal or deemed disposal of certain assets.

The assets in respect of which you can claim these deductions include:

- qualified small business corporation shares.
- qualified farm property.
- qualified fishing property.

If you believe you are entitled to receive any of the above deductions, you should seek advice from your tax advisor.

Important Note

The information provided in this tax section is only a basic overview of capital gains tax in Canada. For further information, visit the Canada Revenue Agency's website (www.cra.gc) or speak to your tax advisor.

A Special Request – Please Leave a Review on Amazon

Thank you for purchasing this Last Will & Testament Kit.

Your positive book review could really help us and help other customers make informed decisions when purchasing self-help kits like this one.

This link will take you to the Amazon.co.uk review page for this book. We would be very grateful if you could please leave a positive 5 Star Review.

Estate-bee.com/review30

Getting Ready to Make Your Own Will

Do I Need a Lawyer?

The short answer is "no". You are free to draft your own will without hiring a lawyer or legal advisor. If your situation is not a complicated one, and you simply want to make gifts, appoint guardians and executors, etc., under your will, then preparing your own will should not be very difficult provided that you have some good self-help materials to hand. However, if your situation is complex or is unusual in some way, you should, at the very least, consult a lawyer.

Deciding on Your Beneficiaries

The first thing you need to do when making a will is to make some lists. You will need to list some or all of the following items:-

- your objectives in distributing your estate;

- your assets and liabilities;

- family members whom you wish to benefit under your will;

- friends and others that you would like to benefit under your will – maybe you want to make a gift to your faithful housekeeper of many years or the friend who's stood by you through all your highs and lows, for example;

- the relationship between you and each of the beneficiaries (this helps for identification purposes);

- charities that you wish to make a gift to; and

- list the particular items, or cash amounts, that you want each beneficiary to receive.

Once you have made your lists and decided on who is to receive cash or specific gifts, you should also consider the balance or residuary of your estate. Do this, even if you think you've distributed everything you possess already. Decide on who will receive that and, if more than one person, the percentage share that each will receive.

To help you make the above lists, we have included a Will Writing Worksheet at the back of this kit. You can write on the pages in this kit or, alternatively, download the form directly from **www.estate-bee.com**.

Once you have decided on the people and organizations that will receive your assets, the next step will be for you to decide on who will act as your executors.

Deciding on Who to Appoint as Your Executors

Unless your estate is very large and complex, two people will be sufficient to act as the executors of your estate. A spouse, son, daughter or other close family member is usually the best place to start when choosing an executor, or failing any of them being willing or suitable, a close and trusted friend. The second executor/executrix might be another son or daughter, your (preferably younger) sibling, or your lawyer or accountant. Of course, you are free to appoint only one executor if you prefer.

Again, before appointing an executor, be sure to ask whether they would be willing and able to take on the role.

Deciding on Who to Appoint Guardians of Your Minor Children

If you have minor children, you should appoint a guardian for your children – even if your spouse is still alive. The clause will say something like "If my wife Mary (or "husband John") predeceases me then I appoint John Smith as testamentary guardian of my minor children'. Keep in mind that the guardian you appoint must be an adult. In practice, it's common to appoint one's brother or sister and their spouse to take on this role together, provided they are willing and able to do so. In the case of a young family, the children's grandparents might be a natural choice for guardians.

Decide What Type of Will You Need

Review the descriptions of the wills in Appendix 3 and choose the will which best describes your circumstances. Then print your chosen will and complete it in accordance with the instructions in Appendix 4 and Appendix 5.

Choosing People to Witness You Signing Your Will

The laws in most provinces provide that in order for a will to be valid two people must witness the testator sign the will. In order for a person to act as a witness to the testator's signing of the will, they must have reached the age of majority in the testator's province of residence and should not be a beneficiary under the will (or the spouse of any such beneficiary). If a beneficiary under a will (or their spouse for that matter) acts as a witness then the gift to the beneficiary will be deemed to be void. The will, however, will otherwise remain valid.

Singing Your Will

The laws of each province set out the formal requirements for executing a will. In general, your will must be executed in the following manner:-

- you must first sign your name, using a pen, in the space provided for signature on the final page of your will; and

- each of your chosen witnesses must then, in your presence and in the presence of each other, write his/her name, address and occupation in the space provided on the final page of the will and also sign their name with their normal signature.

In the province of Quebec both the testator and the two witnesses must initial each page of the will. While this is not mandatory in the rest of Canada, it is a good idea to have all pages initialed even if it is not a requirement.

Did You Know

Generally, a will must be signed by you or by someone directed to do so on your behalf. Signatures may include marks, initials, a rubber stamp, a 'nick-name' or even a former name.

After You Have Made Your Will....

Where to Store Your Will

Once your will has been properly executed, place it in a safe place that is accessible to your executors after your death. Make sure a close friend, relative or your executor knows where to find your will and how to get access to it when the time comes. If you had a lawyer prepare your will, it would be useful to have him or her retain the original in their strong room or safe, or even retain a copy with a note stating where the original can be found.

Just don't be too clever! The last thing you want is a will hunt, especially if you have made and revoked a number of wills, and no one is sure of the date of your most recent one!

Keeping Your Will Updated

In drafting your will, it's important to understand that events will most likely occur in your lifetime which will give rise to a need to change the provisions of your will. These events may come around as a result of changes in the law, your financial circumstances, the value of your assets and even in your preferences in relation to beneficiaries. If your will is not updated to address these changes, they can have significant unintended consequences – particularly in respect of the manner in which your assets are ultimately divided amongst your family and friends.

Important Note

Changes in your circumstances can affect your distribution plans. Perhaps,

- you remarried and 'inherited' a new stepchild or two. Yet neither your new spouse nor your stepchildren are mentioned in your will.

- you left various blocks of shares to different children. One block has more than doubled in value, while another is practically worthless with the primary company in the portfolio going into liquidation. Yet you meant your children to share more or less equally.

- a small parcel of land you left to your cousin has suddenly quadrupled in price due to a new shopping centre project getting the go-ahead. The value of their inheritance may be far more than you intended to leave them.

- you sold a valuable painting you had earmarked for one of your grandchildren? Unless you substitute a different bequest, that grandchild might end up inheriting nothing.

Suddenly your bequests are way out of balance. If this happens, it's time to update your will.

Some typical changes in circumstances that can cause unintended consequences if not addressed include:

- birth of new family members;

- death of intended beneficiaries;

- significant changes in beneficiaries' circumstances;

- changes in your relationships (such as marriage or divorce);

- acquisition of new assets;

- substantial appreciation in value of particular existing assets; and

- disposal or substantial depreciation in value or loss of certain existing assets.

In order to make sure that changes in your circumstances are addressed in your will it is recommended that you review and update your will annually or at the very least, every three years. It's also recommended that you review your will on the occurrence of any significant change in your personal circumstances such as in the cases of the examples set out above.

Using a Codicil to Update or Change Your Will

You are free to change the terms of your will including the beneficiaries named in it whenever you like. Of course, you do need to be careful when dealing with spouses and children due to their legal rights. Fortunately, amending your will is relatively straightforward. To amend a will, you can either make a new will in its entirety or you can make a codicil which will amend a specific portion of your existing will.

A codicil is simply a testamentary document that amends rather than replaces an existing will. It requires exactly the same formalities as to execution as does a will. You can use different witnesses, but it's better (if they can be easily found) to use the same people who witnessed the original will. Once the codicil has been executed, it should be placed with the original will for safe keeping.

Similar to the position with wills, a witness to a codicil should not be a beneficiary under the codicil, as this will preclude them from inheriting under the codicil.

Resource

Full details on how to prepare a codicil are contained in our kit entitled "Codicil to a Last Will and Testament Kit". For your immediate copy, simply visit www.estate-bee.com.

Revoking Your Will

If you need to revoke your will for any reason, you may do so in several ways:

- draft a new will (which will usually contain a statement that all old wills are revoked);

- physically destroy your old will by tearing it up or burning it;

- a will can be revoked by marriage or the signing of a civil partnership agreement unless your will was drafted "in contemplation of marriage" or "in contemplation of the civil partnership". Quebec does not have this specific rule while New Brunswick, Ontario and Nova Scotia have rules that may save a will made prior to marriage. So, you should not assume that your will is automatically invalidated by marriage or a new civil partnership; and

- where you have a child after signing the will, your will may be revoked if you have not dealt with this possibility in your will.

Important Note

The writing of the word 'revoked' on a will is insufficient to legally revoke the will.

A separation or divorce does not ordinarily invalidate your Will. In most provinces (except Alberta, New Brunswick, and Newfoundland), where a couple are divorced, the spouse is deemed to have predeceased the testator for purposes of accepting the appointment of executor and in respect of any gifts to that spouse. Similar legislation has also been passed in Nova Scotia; while in Quebec, divorce revokes bequests made to a spouse unless the testator has provided otherwise.

Similar to divorce, the end of an adult interdependent relationship does not automatically invalidate a Will.

For the avoidance of doubt, you should always consider updating your will after you divorce or separate from your partner.

Appendices

Appendix 1

Glossary of Legal Terms

This glossary is designed to help you understand some of the more common legal terms you may encounter when making your will.

Term	Definition
Administration	The process by which an administrator oversees the distribution of your estate and deals with the payment of any outstanding debts owing by you if you die intestate.
Administrator	This is the person who is designated by the courts to oversee the administration.
Adoption	The process of legally adopting a child into your care thereby creating a parent-child relationship. A legally adopted child may have rights of inheritance in the estate of his/her adoptive parent(s) but not always in the estate of his or her natural parent(s).
Adult	This is a person who has reached the age of majority in his or her province.
Assets	All possessions of yours including insurance policies and rights to receive other assets/money.
Beneficiary	A person or organization who will inherit part or all of your assets or estate under a will, trust or on intestacy.
Bequest	A gift of personal property under a will.
Children	The term extends to include legitimate, illegitimate and adopted children. Stepchildren are often excluded from the meaning of this

term and should therefore, for the avoidance of doubt, be expressly mentioned in your will or trust if you wish them to benefit.

Codicil
A codicil acts to make an amendment to your will and is legally binding once all legal formalities have been complied with.

Deceased/Decedent
The person who has died.

Devise
This is a gift of immovable property (also known as real property) such as land or buildings made under a will.

Discretionary Trust
This is a trust which gives power to the trustees to administer the trust assets at their own discretion.

Disponer
The person making a gift of property under a will.

Disinherit
To exclude someone who is rightfully entitled to inherit something from your estate from an inheritance.

Domicile
Your domicile is the country where you believe that your home is and, if you are not there now, where you intend, eventually, to return. You might live temporarily, or even for extended periods of years, away from your country of domicile but if your intention is to return to that place you retain it as your place of domicile. Once you have decided to settle permanently in another country your domicile changes.

Donee
The person receiving a gift.

Donor
The person making a gift.

Estate
The term "estate" refers to everything you own at the time of your death – all assets, real and personal, less your liabilities.

Executor/ Executrix
This is the person or persons nominated or appointed by you in your will to deal with the administration and distribution of your estate following your death. Executor is the masculine term whereas

executrix is the feminine term. Sometimes, executors are called personal representatives.

Fiduciary

A fiduciary is someone who has undertaken to act for and on behalf of another person in a particular matter in circumstances which give rise to a relationship of trust and confidence. Examples include trustees, executors, and guardians.

Fiduciary Duty

Fiduciary duties are duties that the executor or trustee owes to the beneficiaries of the estate whose assets the executor or trustee has control over. These duties include a duty to act in good faith for the benefit of the beneficiaries.

Gift

A gift or a present is the transfer of something without the need for compensation and without any obligation on the part of the donor to make the gift.

Guardian

A legal guardian is a person who has the legal authority (and the corresponding duty) to care for the personal and property interests of a minor or an incapacitated person. In the case of minors, you can appoint a guardian under your will to care for your children following your death. However, this appointment must ultimately be approved by the court.

Heir

A person who is entitled either by law or by the terms of a will or trust to inherit the estate of another.

Inherit

To receive something, by legal succession or bequest, after the previous owner's death.

Intestate/Intestacy

Where you die without making a valid will to deal with the distribution of your estate you are said to have died intestate. Where this happens, intestacy proceedings will be instituted whereby the court will appoint an administrator to distribute your estate and pay your debts in accordance with the law. These laws are known as the rules of 'intestacy'.

Intestate Succession

The order in which people inherit property when someone dies intestate.

Issue	The immediate descendants of a person.
Legacy	A gift made in a will.
Legatee	A person who receives a legacy.
Minor	A child who has not yet reached the age of majority.
Per stirpes	A "per stirpes" arrangement means that if a beneficiary/heir predeceases the testator/intestate leaving a child then that child takes the share that his parent would have been entitled to receive had the parent been alive. Where there is more than one child, that share is divided equally amongst the children.
Personal Property	Physical assets that are not fixed permanently to real estate. It includes mobile property like furniture, equipment, vehicles, collectibles and inventory for example.
Personal Representative	Another name for an executor.
Primary Beneficiary	This is the person who stands first in line to receive a gift under a will or trust. Should the primary beneficiary die before becoming entitled to receive a gift under a will or trust, the gift will pass to an alternate beneficiary (if one is named) or revert to the residuary beneficiary if no alternate is named.
Probate	Probate has come to mean not just proving the validity of a last will and testament but the entire administrative process involving the collecting of assets, payment of debts and the passing of a deceased person's legal title to property to his or her beneficiaries. If the deceased person has not made a will, this process will be known as an administration rather than a probate.
Residue/Remainder	The remainder of a testator's estate after all specific gifts have been made under the testator's will, and after all of the testator's debts have been paid.

Residuary Beneficiary	The person who will receive the residue of the testator's estate. The residue can also be divided between more than one person.
Real Property	Land and generally whatever is erected upon or affixed to it.
Spouse	The person to whom you are married - not a cohabitee.
Surviving Spouse	The husband or wife that remains alive after the death of the other spouse.
Survivorship	The right of a person to secure ownership of an asset (such as land, real estate, bank accounts, etc.) by reason of the fact that this person has outlived the other joint owners.
Testamentary Trust	A trust created under the terms of a will.
Testate	A person who has died leaving a valid will providing for the distribution of his assets.
Testator/Testatrix	This means the man/woman who makes a will.
Trust	A trust is a relationship of reliance whereby one party requests another party to manage property on his or her behalf, or on behalf of another in accordance with a specific set of rules. The persons who are charged with the management of the property are known as trustees.
Trustee	The person or persons who have been appointed to look after property that is held in trust. The trustees are not allowed to do anything with the property unless the terms of the trust allow it. The trustees owe a number of fiduciary duties to the beneficiaries of the trust property concerned.
Will	A legal document setting out a person's wishes regarding the disposal of his or her property after death.

Appendix 2

Will Writing Worksheet

Downloadable Forms

Blank copies of this form can be downloaded from the EstateBee website. Simply login to your account or, if you don't have an account, you can create one for free.

www.estate-bee.com/login

Once logged in, go to your profile page and enter the code listed below in the 'Use Codes' tab:

WorksheetCAN21

Will Writing Worksheet

Will Writing Worksheet

Before you begin the process of making a will, we recommend that you print out this worksheet and complete it as appropriate. It will help you to work out what assets you own, and identify your liabilities, before deciding who you would like to make gifts to and how. By having all the relevant details at your fingertips, it will save a considerable amount of time in the preparation of your estate planning documents.

The document is also useful for document your choice of fiduciaries such as executors, trustees, healthcare agents, etc.

In addition, by keeping this worksheet with your will and other personal papers, it will greatly assist your executor in identifying and locating your assets and liabilities when the time comes.

Personal Information	You	Your Spouse
Full Name:		
Birth Date:		
Social Security Number:		
Occupation:		
Work Telephone:		
Work Fax:		
Mobile/Pager:		
Email Address:		
Home Address (Include County):		
Home Telephone:		
Home Fax:		
Date and Place of Marriage:		

Maiden name of spouse:		
If either of you were previously married, list the dates of prior marriage, name of previous spouse, names of living children from prior marriage(s), and state whether marriage ended by death or divorce:		
Location of Safe Deposit Box (if any):		

Notification of Death
(On my death, please notify the following persons)

Full Name	Telephone	Address

Children (Living)

Full Name	Address (If child does not reside with you)	Birth Date

Children (Deceased)

Full Name		

Grandchildren

Full Name	Address	Birth Date

Parents

Full Name	Address	Telephone Number

Brothers and Sisters		
Full Name	Address	Telephone Number

Assets		
Description & Location	Current Fair Market Value	How is Title Held?
Real Estate (Land and Buildings)		
Closely Held Companies, Businesses, Partnerships etc.		

Bank Accounts		
Shares, Bonds and Mutual Funds		
Vehicles, Boats, etc.		

Other Property		
Total		

Liabilities	
Description	Amount
Mortgages	
Loans	
Debts	

Other Liabilities	
Total	

Life Insurance and Annuities

Company	Insured	Beneficiary(ies)	Face Amount	Cash Value
Total				

Pensions and Other Retirement Plans

Company Custodian	Participant	Type of Plan	Vested Amount	Death Benefit

Total				

Distribution Plan
(Describe in general terms how you wish to leave your property at death)

Other Beneficiaries
(Information about persons other than your spouse and family members who you wish to benefit)

Full Name	Age	Address	Relationship to You

Fiduciaries
(List name, address and home telephone for each person)

	Full Name	Address	Telephone Number
Last Will and Testament			
Primary Executor:			
First Alternate Executor:			
Second Alternate Executor:			
Primary Trustee:			
First Alternate Trustee:			

Second Alternate Trustee:			
Guardian of Minor Children:			
First Alternate Guardian:			
Second Alternate Guardian:			
Discretionary Trust			
Successor Trustee:			
First Alternate Successor Trustee:			
Second Alternate Successor Trustee:			
Agent under a Power of Attorney **for Finance and Property (Enduring Power of Attorney)**			
Agent:			
First Alternate Agent:			
Second Alternate Agent:			
Agent under a Healthcare Power of Attorney (Healthcare)			
Healthcare Agent:			
First Alternate Healthcare Agent:			

Second Alternate Healthcare Agent:			
Living Will			
Healthcare Agent:			
First Alternate Healthcare Agent:			
Second Alternate Healthcare Agent:			

Advisors

(List name, address and home telephone for each person)

	Full Name	Address	Telephone Number
Lawyer			
Accountant			
Financial Advisor			
Stockbroker			
Insurance Agent			
Other Information:			

Document Locations

Description	Location	Other Information

Last Will & Testament		
Trust Agreement		
Living Will		
Healthcare Power of Attorney		
Power of Attorney for Finance and Property		
Title Deeds		
Leases		
Share Certificates		
Mortgage Documents		
Birth Certificate		
Marriage Certificate		
Divorce Decree		
Donor Cards		
Other Documents		

Funeral Plan

(Describe in general terms what funeral and burial arrangements you would like to have)

Appendix 3

Sample Wills

A Special Request –
Please Leave a Review on Amazon

Thank you for purchasing this Last Will & Testament Kit.

Your positive book review could really help us and help other customers make informed decisions when purchasing self-help kits like this one.

This link will take you to the Amazon.co.uk review page for this book. We would be very grateful if you could please leave a positive 5 Star Review.

Estate-bee.com/review30

Sample Wills

First Will & Second Will

Unmarried and not in a civil partnership, with no children

These are "Simple Wills" and are used where a person is unmarried and does not have any children. The Will is used to appoint an executor and to pass your estate to designated persons of your choice.

The First Will should be used where you have one intended beneficiary for the residue of your estate.

The Second Will should be used where you have more than one intended beneficiary for the residue of your estate.

Third Will

Unmarried and not in a civil partnership, with children

This will is for use by a person who is unmarried and has children. A trust will be created for the benefit of your children with power for the trustees to provide for your children until they reach a specific age (usually 18 or 21 years). Thereafter the residuary of your estate will be divided equally between your children.

Fourth Will & Fifth Will

Married or in a civil partnership with adult children

These wills are for use by married couples with adult children. In these wills, each spouse leaves their estate to the other with a provision that, should the surviving spouse die within a period of 30 days of the other spouse, the entire estate will pass to a different named beneficiary.

The Fourth Will is for use by a husband. The Fifth Will is for use by a wife.

Sixth Will & Seventh Will

Married or in a civil partnership with minor children

These Wills are for use by married couples with minor children. In these wills, each spouse leaves their estate to the other with a provision that, should they both die within a period of 30 days of each other the entire estate will pass to the trustees of the estate to hold same on trust for the benefit of their minor children.

The Sixth Will is for use by a husband. The Seventh Will is for use by a wife.

Eighth Will & Ninth Will

Married or in a civil partnership with no children

These wills are for use by couples who are married or in a civil domestic partnership and who do not have any living children. In these wills, each spouse/partner leaves their estate to the other with a provision that, should the surviving spouse/partner die within a period of 30 days of the other spouse/partner, the entire estate will pass to a different named beneficiary.

The Eighth Will is for use by a husband or male partner. The Ninth Will is for use by a wife or female partner.

FIRST WILL

(Unmarried and not in a civil partnership, with no children, single beneficiary)

Downloadable Forms

Blank copies of this form can be downloaded from the EstateBee website. Simply login to your account or, if you don't have an account, you can create one for free.

www.estate-bee.com/login

Once logged in, go to your profile page and enter the code listed below in the 'Use Codes' tab:

FirstWillCAN21

LAST WILL AND TESTAMENT

OF

_____

THIS IS THE LAST WILL AND TESTAMENT OF _____, of
_____, in the province of _____.

1. I hereby **REVOKE** all former wills, codicils and other testamentary dispositions at any time heretofore made by me and declare this to be my last will.

2. I am not married, nor do I have a registered civil partner. I do not have any living children.

3. I appoint _____ of _____ to be executor and trustee of this my will. If this person or institution shall for any reason be unable or unwilling to act (at any time) as my executor, then I appoint _____ of _____ _____ to be executor and trustee of my will. The expression "executor" wherever used in this my will shall, unless otherwise stated, mean the person or persons from time to time acting in the office of executor and trustee of this my will, and wherever the singular or masculine are used throughout this will, the same shall be construed as meaning the plural or feminine or body corporate (and vice versa) where the context so requires.

4. I direct my executor to pay all my just debts (which are capable of enforcement against me), funeral and testamentary expenses as soon as practical after my death.

5. I give, devise, and bequeath _____ to _____ of _____ absolutely.

6. I give, devise, and bequeath _____ to _____ of _____ absolutely.

[Repeat or delete as necessary to make further specific gifts/bequests. Note you may need to renumber subsequent clauses]

7. As to all the rest, residue, and remainder of my estate of whatsoever nature and wheresoever situate I give devise and bequeath the same to _____ of _____ _____. However, if this person predeceases me, then I give devise and bequeath all the rest, residue, and remainder of my estate to _____ of _____.

8. In addition to all statutory powers and common law powers of executors and trustees and special powers herein conferred, my executor shall have the powers set out below:

(a) to dispose of any property or any interest therein at such times and upon such terms and conditions and in such manner as shall seem proper and to give good and sufficient instruments of transfer and to receive the proceeds of any such disposition;

(b) to invest or apply the estate or trust estate or any part thereof in any way whatsoever in which a man of ordinary prudence would invest or apply his own funds including power to borrow or lend with or without security;

(c) to purchase, manage, maintain and insure any property and to lease the same for such periods and on such terms as shall seem advantageous, and if advisable to pay for the value of any improvements made by a tenant under any such lease; to incur, extend or renew mortgage indebtedness; to make ordinary and extraordinary repairs and alterations to any building, to raze or erect buildings and to make improvements or to abandon any buildings or property; and to make any agreement of partition of such property and to give or receive money or other property in connection therewith;

(d) to keep property insured against such risks (if any) and for such amount as my executor shall in his/her absolute discretion think fit (but so that my executor shall not in any way be obliged to effect any insurance and shall not be liable for any failure to insure) with some insurance office of repute in the name of my executor and my executor may for such purpose pay all premiums and other costs incurred in connection with such insurance out of any money held upon the same trusts under this will or any codicil to it as such insured property (and so that the benefit of any such insurance shall be held upon the like trusts);

(e) to exercise or sell all rights, options, powers, and privileges, and to vote in person or by proxy, in relation to any stocks, bonds or other securities, all as fully as might be done by persons owning similar property in their own right;

(f) to assent to, oppose and participate in any reorganization, recapitalization, merger, consolidation or similar proceeding, to deposit securities, delegate discretionary powers, pay assessments or other expenses and exchange property, all as fully as might be done by persons owning similar property in their own right;

(g) to manage, sell, administer, liquidate, continue, or otherwise deal with any corporation, partnership or other business interest received by my trust estate as my executor deems fit;

(h) to borrow money and pledge or mortgage any property as security therefore;

(i) to institute, defend, settle, or compromise, by arbitration or otherwise, all claims;

(j) to employ or retain such agents and advisors, including any firm with which any fiduciary may be affiliated, as may seem advisable and to delegate authority thereto, and to compensate them from the funds of my estate provided such compensation is reasonable in the circumstances;

(k) to settle any entitlement of any beneficiary, in part or in whole, by payment in cash or by the transfer of a specific asset or assets to the beneficiary or to the legal guardian of the beneficiary with power to require the beneficiary or any such guardian to accept such asset or assets at such value or estimate of value as my executor shall (acting reasonably) unilaterally deem fair;

(l) where my executor is authorized or required to pay a pecuniary legacy to any person who does not have the capacity to give a valid receipt for it my executor may pay the same to any parent or guardian of such person for the benefit of such person without seeing to the application of it or himself/herself apply the same for the benefit of such person as may be directed in writing by such parent or guardian and the receipt of such parent or guardian shall be a sufficient discharge to my executor;

(m) the receipt of the person professing to be the treasurer or other proper officer of any charity to which any legacy may be payable under this will shall be a sufficient discharge to my executor;

(n) to pay all necessary or proper expenses and charges from income or principal, or partly from each, in such manner as may seem equitable.

9. **I DECLARE** that any executor and/or trustee (if any) for the time being of this my will or of any codicil hereto who is a lawyer or engaged in any other profession shall be entitled to make and receive in all such charges and emoluments for business whether of an ordinary professional or other character done by him or any partner of his in relation to the administration of my estate or the execution of the trusts of this my will or any codicil hereto as he would have been entitled to make and receive in respect of such business if he had not been an executor and/or trustee.

10. **I DECLARE** that no executor or trustee of this will shall be liable for any loss not attributable to their own dishonesty or to the willful commission by them of any act known to be a breach of their duties and obligations as executor or trustee.

IN WITNESS HEREOF I have to this my Last Will and Testament, written upon this and the preceding pages, subscribed my name this _____ day of _____ 20 ____.

_____
(Signed)

Signed by the above-named testator as and for his/her Last Will and Testament in our presence, each of us being present at the same time who at his/her request and in his/her presence and in the presence of each other have hereunto subscribed our names as witnesses.

Name: _____

Signature: _____

Address: _____

_____

_____

_____

Occupation: _____

Name: _____

Signature: _____

Address: _____

_____

_____

_____

Occupation: _____

SECOND WILL

(Unmarried and not in a civil partnership with no children, multiple beneficiaries)

Downloadable Forms

Blank copies of this form can be downloaded from the EstateBee website. Simply login to your account or, if you don't have an account, you can create one for free.

www.estate-bee.com/login

Once logged in, go to your profile page and enter the code listed below in the 'Use Codes' tab:

SecondWillCAN21

LAST WILL AND TESTAMENT

OF

_____

THIS IS THE LAST WILL AND TESTAMENT OF _____, of
_____, in the province of _____.

1. I hereby **REVOKE** all former wills, codicils and other testamentary dispositions at any time
    heretofore made by me and declare this to be my last will.

2. I am not married, nor do I have a registered civil partner. I do not have any living children.

3. I appoint _____ of _____ to be executor and trustee
    of this my will. If this person or institution shall for any reason be unable or unwilling to act
    (at any time) as my executor, then I appoint _____ of _____
    _____ to be executor and trustee of my will. The expression "executor" wherever used in this
    my will shall, unless otherwise stated, mean the person or persons from time to time acting in
    the office of executor and trustee of this my will, and wherever the singular or masculine are
    used throughout this will, the same shall be construed as meaning the plural or feminine or
    body corporate (and vice versa) where the context so requires.

4. I direct my executor to pay all my just debts (which are capable of enforcement against me),
    funeral and testamentary expenses as soon as practical after my death.

5. I give, devise, and bequeath _____ to _____
    _____ of _____ absolutely.

6. I give, devise, and bequeath _____ to _____
    _____ of _____ absolutely.

_[Repeat or delete as necessary to make further specific gifts/bequests. Note you may need to renumber
subsequent clauses]_

7. I give, devise, and bequeath all the rest, residue and remainder of my estate to _____
    _____ of _____and _____
    _____ of _____ in equal
    shares. However, in the event that either of the above persons predecease me, then I give,
    devise and bequeath their share of my estate to _____ of
    _____.

8. In addition to all statutory powers and common law powers of executors and trustees and
    special powers herein conferred, my executor shall have the powers set out below:

(a) to dispose of any property or any interest therein at such times and upon such terms
    and conditions and in such manner as shall seem proper and to give good and sufficient
    instruments of transfer and to receive the proceeds of any such disposition;

(b) to invest or apply the estate or trust estate or any part thereof in any way whatsoever in
    which a man of ordinary prudence would invest or apply his own funds including power to
    borrow or lend with or without security;

(c) to purchase, manage, maintain and insure any property and to lease the same for such periods
    and on such terms as shall seem advantageous, and if advisable to pay for the value of any
    improvements made by a tenant under any such lease; to incur, extend or renew mortgage
    indebtedness; to make ordinary and extraordinary repairs and alterations to any building, to
    raze or erect buildings and to make improvements or to abandon any buildings or property;
    and to make any agreement of partition of such property and to give or receive money or
    other property in connection therewith;

(d) to keep property insured against such risks (if any) and for such amount as my executor
    shall in his/her absolute discretion think fit (but so that my executor shall not in any way be
    obliged to effect any insurance and shall not be liable for any failure to insure) with some
    insurance office of repute in the name of my executor and my executor may for such purpose
    pay all premiums and other costs incurred in connection with such insurance out of any
    money held upon the same trusts under this will or any codicil to it as such insured property
    (and so that the benefit of any such insurance shall be held upon the like trusts);

(e) to exercise or sell all rights, options, powers, and privileges, and to vote in person or by proxy, in relation to any stocks, bonds or other securities, all as fully as might be done by persons owning similar property in their own right;

(f) to assent to, oppose and participate in any reorganization, recapitalization, merger, consolidation, or similar proceeding, to deposit securities, delegate discretionary powers, pay assessments or other expenses and exchange property, all as fully as might be done by persons owning similar property in their own right;

(g) to manage, sell, administer, liquidate, continue, or otherwise deal with any corporation, partnership or other business interest received by my trust estate as my executor deems fit;

(h) to borrow money and pledge or mortgage any property as security therefore;

(i) to institute, defend, settle, or compromise, by arbitration or otherwise, all claims;

(j) to employ or retain such agents and advisors, including any firm with which any fiduciary may be affiliated, as may seem advisable and to delegate authority thereto, and to compensate them from the funds of my estate provided such compensation is reasonable in the circumstances;

(k) to settle any entitlement of any beneficiary, in part or in whole, by payment in cash or by the transfer of a specific asset or assets to the beneficiary or to the legal guardian of the beneficiary with power to require the beneficiary or any such guardian to accept such asset or assets at such value or estimate of value as my executor shall (acting reasonably) unilaterally deem fair;

(l) where my executor is authorized or required to pay a pecuniary legacy to any person who does not have the capacity to give a valid receipt for it my executor may pay the same to any parent or guardian of such person for the benefit of such person without seeing to the application of it or himself/herself apply the same for the benefit of such person as may be directed in writing by such parent or guardian and the receipt of such parent or guardian shall be a sufficient discharge to my executor;

(m) the receipt of the person professing to be the treasurer or other proper officer of any charity to which any legacy may be payable under this will shall be a sufficient discharge to my executor; and

(n) to pay all necessary or proper expenses and charges from income or principal, or partly from each, in such manner as may seem equitable.

.   **I DECLARE** that any executor and/or trustee (if any) for the time being of this my will or of any codicil hereto who is a lawyer or engaged in any other profession shall be entitled to make and receive in all such charges and emoluments for business whether of an ordinary professional or other character done by him or any partner of his in relation to the administration of my estate or the execution of the trusts of this my will or any codicil hereto as he would have been entitled to make and receive in respect of such business if he had not been an executor and/or trustee.

10. **I DECLARE** that no executor or trustee of this will shall be liable for any loss not attributable to their own dishonesty or to the willful commission by them of any act known to be a breach of their duties and obligations as executor or trustee.

IN WITNESS HEREOF I have to this my Last Will and Testament, written upon this and the preceding pages, subscribed my name this ____ day of _____ 20__.

_____

(Signed)

Signed by the above-named testator as and for his/her Last Will and Testament in our presence, each of us being present at the same time who at his/her request and in his/her presence and in the presence of each other have hereunto subscribed our names as witnesses.

Name: _____

Signature: _____

Address: _____

              _____

              _____

              _____

Occupation: _____

Name: _____

Signature: _____

Address: _____

_____

_____

_____

Occupation: _____

THIRD WILL

(Unmarried and not in a civil partnership, with children)

LAST WILL AND TESTAMENT

OF

_____

THIS IS THE LAST WILL AND TESTAMENT OF _____, of _____
_____, in the province of _____.

1. I hereby **REVOKE** all former wills, codicils and other testamentary dispositions at any time heretofore made by me and declare this to be my last will.

2. I am not married, nor do I have a registered civil partner. I have _____ child/children namely _____.

3. I appoint _____ of _____ to be executor and trustee of this my will. If this person or institution shall for any reason be unable or unwilling to act (at any time) as my executor, then I appoint _____ of _____ _____ to be executor and trustee of my will. The expression "executor" wherever used in this my will shall, unless otherwise stated, mean the person or persons from time to time acting in the office of executor and trustee of this my will, and wherever the singular or masculine are used throughout this will, the same shall be construed as meaning the plural or feminine or body corporate (and vice versa) where the context so requires.

4. I direct my executor to pay all my just debts (which are capable of enforcement against me), funeral and testamentary expenses as soon as practical after my death.

5. I appoint _____ of _____ and _____ _____ of _____ guardians of my infant children and conservators of the estate of each of my infant children, to serve as such without bond.

6. I give, devise, and bequeath _____ to _____ of ___ _____ absolutely.

7. I give, devise, and bequeath _____ to _____ of __
    _____ absolutely.

[Repeat or delete as necessary to make further specific gifts/bequests. Note you may need to renumber subsequent clauses]

8. I give, devise, and bequeath to my executor all the rest, residue and remainder of my estate upon trust to hold the same or the proceeds of sale thereof as trustee and to divide the same among such of my children as shall survive me and reach the age of _____ years and if more than one in equal shares absolutely BUT if any child of mine dies before me or before attaining a vested interest leaving a child or children then such child or children shall on reaching the age of _____ years take per stirpes the share which his/her parent would otherwise have taken and if more than one in equal shares absolutely.

9. In addition to all statutory powers and common law powers of executors and trustees and special powers herein conferred, my executor shall have the powers set out below:

(a) to dispose of any property or any interest therein at such times and upon such terms and conditions and in such manner as shall seem proper and to give good and sufficient instruments of transfer and to receive the proceeds of any such disposition;

(b) to invest or apply the estate or trust estate or any part thereof in any way whatsoever in which a man of ordinary prudence would invest or apply his own funds including power to borrow or lend with or without security;

(c) to purchase, manage, maintain and insure any property and to lease the same for such periods and on such terms as shall seem advantageous, and if advisable to pay for the value of any improvements made by a tenant under any such lease; to incur, extend or renew mortgage indebtedness; to make ordinary and extraordinary repairs and alterations to any building, to raze or erect buildings and to make improvements or to abandon any buildings or property; and to make any agreement of partition of such property and to give or receive money or other property in connection therewith;

(d) to keep property insured against such risks (if any) and for such amount as my executor shall in his/her absolute discretion think fit (but so that my executor shall not in any way be obliged to effect any insurance and shall not be liable for any failure to insure) with some insurance office of repute in the name of my executor and my executor may for such purpose pay all premiums and other costs incurred in connection with such insurance out of any money held upon the same trusts under this will or any codicil to it as such insured property (and so that the benefit of any such insurance shall be held upon the like trusts);

(e)   to exercise or sell all rights, options, powers, and privileges, and to vote in person or by proxy, in relation to any stocks, bonds or other securities, all as fully as might be done by persons owning similar property in their own right;

(f)   to assent to, oppose and participate in any reorganization, recapitalization, merger, consolidation, or similar proceeding, to deposit securities, delegate discretionary powers, pay assessments or other expenses and exchange property, all as fully as might be done by persons owning similar property in their own right;

(g)   to manage, sell, administer, liquidate, continue, or otherwise deal with any corporation, partnership or other business interest received by my trust estate as my executor deems fit;

(h)   to borrow money and pledge or mortgage any property as security therefore;

(i)   to institute, defend, settle, or compromise, by arbitration or otherwise, all claims;

(j)   to employ or retain such agents and advisors, including any firm with which any fiduciary may be affiliated, as may seem advisable and to delegate authority thereto, and to compensate them from the funds of my estate provided such compensation is reasonable in the circumstances;

(k)   to settle any entitlement of any beneficiary, in part or in whole, by payment in cash or by the transfer of a specific asset or assets to the beneficiary or to the legal guardian of the beneficiary with power to require the beneficiary or any such guardian to accept such asset or assets at such value or estimate of value as my executor shall (acting reasonably) unilaterally deem fair;

(l)   where my executor is authorized or required to pay a pecuniary legacy to any person who does not have the capacity to give a valid receipt for it my executor may pay the same to any parent or guardian of such person for the benefit of such person without seeing to the application of it or himself/herself apply the same for the benefit of such person as may be directed in writing by such parent or guardian and the receipt of such parent or guardian shall be a sufficient discharge to my executor;

(m) the receipt of the person professing to be the treasurer or other proper officer of any charity to which any legacy may be payable under this will shall be a sufficient discharge to my executor; and

(n) to pay all necessary or proper expenses and charges from income or principal, or partly from each, in such manner as may seem equitable.

10. **I DECLARE** that any executor and/or trustee (if any) for the time being of this my will or of any codicil hereto who is a lawyer or engaged in any other profession shall be entitled to make and receive in all such charges and emoluments for business whether of an ordinary professional or other character done by him or any partner of his in relation to the administration of my estate or the execution of the trusts of this my will or any codicil hereto as he would have been entitled to make and receive in respect of such business if he had not been an executor and/or trustee.

11. **I DECLARE** that no executor or trustee of this will shall be liable for any loss not attributable to their own dishonesty or to the willful commission by them of any act known to be a breach of their duties and obligations as executor or trustee.

IN WITNESS HEREOF I have to this my Last Will and Testament, written upon this and the preceding pages, subscribed my name this _____ day of _____ 20 _____.

_____

(Signed)

Signed by the above-named testator as and for his/her Last Will and Testament in our presence, each of us being present at the same time who at his/her request and in his/her presence and in the presence of each other have hereunto subscribed our names as witnesses.

Name: _____

Signature: _____

Address: _____

_____

_____

_____

Occupation: _____

Name: _____

Signature: _____

Address: _____

_____

_____

_____

Occupation: _____

FOURTH WILL

(Married or in a civil partnership with adult children (for husband/male partner))

Downloadable Forms

Blank copies of all this form can be downloaded from the EstateBee website. Simply login to your account or, if you don't have an account, you can create one for free.

www.estate-bee.com/login

Once logged in, go to your profile page and enter the code listed below in the 'Use Codes' tab:

FourthWillCAN21

LAST WILL AND TESTAMENT

OF

_____

THIS IS THE LAST WILL AND TESTAMENT OF _____, of _____
_____, in the province of _____.

1. I hereby **REVOKE** all former wills, codicils and other testamentary dispositions at any time heretofore made by me and declare this to be my last will.

2. [I am married to _____.]/[I am in a registered civil partnership with _____ _____.] I have _____ child/children namely _____.

3. I appoint _____ of _____ to be executor and trustee of this my will. If this person or institution shall for any reason be unable or unwilling to act (at any time) as my executor, then I appoint _____ of _____ _____ to be executor and trustee of my will. The expression "executor" wherever used in this my will shall, unless otherwise stated, mean the person or persons from time to time acting in the office of executor and trustee of this my will, and wherever the singular or masculine are used throughout this will, the same shall be construed as meaning the plural or feminine or body corporate (and vice versa) where the context so requires.

4. I direct my executor to pay all my just debts (which are capable of enforcement against me), funeral and testamentary expenses as soon as practical after my death.

5. I give, devise, and bequeath _____ to _____ of ____ _____ absolutely.

6. I give, devise, and bequeath _____ to _____ _of _____ absolutely.[Repeat or delete as necessary to make further specific gifts/bequests. Note you may need to renumber subsequent clauses]

7. If my wife, _____, shall survive me for a period of one month then

I GIVE, DEVISE AND BEQUEATH all the rest, residue, and remainder of my estate of whatsoever kind and wheresoever situate to my said wife absolutely.

8. If my said wife shall predecease me or shall not survive me for the period aforesaid, I DIRECT that the sixth clause shall not take effect and this my will shall be construed and take effect as if the sixth clause had been wholly omitted therefrom and that the remaining clauses of this will shall take effect.

9. In so far as it may be necessary and for the avoidance of doubt, I direct that if my wife shall survive me for a period of less than one month then the income of my estate accruing from the date of my death until the date of the death of my wife shall be accumulated and form part of my residuary estate.

10. I give, devise, and bequeath all the rest, residue and remainder of my estate to _____ _____ of _____ and _____ _____ of _____in equal shares. However, if either of the above persons predecease me, then I give, devise, and bequeath their share of my estate to _____ _____ of _____.

11. In addition to all statutory powers and common law powers of executors and trustees and special powers herein conferred, my executor shall have the powers set out below:

(a) to dispose of any property or any interest therein at such times and upon such terms and conditions and in such manner as shall seem proper and to give good and sufficient instruments of transfer and to receive the proceeds of any such disposition;

(b) to invest or apply the estate or trust estate or any part thereof in any way whatsoever in which a man of ordinary prudence would invest or apply his own funds including power to borrow or lend with or without security;

(c) to purchase, manage, maintain and insure any property and to lease the same for such periods and on such terms as shall seem advantageous, and if advisable to pay for the value of any improvements made by a tenant under any such lease; to incur, extend or renew mortgage indebtedness; to make ordinary and extraordinary repairs and alterations to any building, to raze or erect buildings and to make improvements or to abandon any buildings or property; and to make any agreement of partition of such property and to give or receive money or other property in connection therewith;

(d)   to keep property insured against such risks (if any) and for such amount as my executor shall in his/her absolute discretion think fit (but so that my executor shall not in any way be obliged to effect any insurance and shall not be liable for any failure to insure) with some insurance office of repute in the name of my executor and my executor may for such purpose pay all premiums and other costs incurred in connection with such insurance out of any money held upon the same trusts under this will or any codicil to it as such insured property (and so that the benefit of any such insurance shall be held upon the like trusts);

(e)   to exercise or sell all rights, options, powers, and privileges, and to vote in person or by proxy, in relation to any stocks, bonds or other securities, all as fully as might be done by persons owning similar property in their own right;

(f)   to assent to, oppose and participate in any reorganization, recapitalization, merger, consolidation, or similar proceeding, to deposit securities, delegate discretionary powers, pay assessments or other expenses and exchange property, all as fully as might be done by persons owning similar property in their own right;

(g)   to manage, sell, administer, liquidate, continue, or otherwise deal with any corporation, partnership or other business interest received by my trust estate as my executor deems fit;

(h)   to borrow money and pledge or mortgage any property as security therefore;

(i)   to institute, defend, settle, or compromise, by arbitration or otherwise, all claims;

(j)   to employ or retain such agents and advisors, including any firm with which any fiduciary may be affiliated, as may seem advisable and to delegate authority thereto, and to compensate them from the funds of my estate provided such compensation is reasonable in the circumstances;

(k)   to settle any entitlement of any beneficiary, in part or in whole, by payment in cash or by the transfer of a specific asset or assets to the beneficiary or to the legal guardian of the beneficiary with power to require the beneficiary or any such guardian to accept such asset or assets at such value or estimate of value as my executor shall (acting reasonably) unilaterally deem fair;

(l)   where my executor is authorized or required to pay a pecuniary legacy to any person who does not have the capacity to give a valid receipt for it my executor may pay the same to any parent or guardian of such person for the benefit of such person without seeing to the application of it or himself/herself apply the same for the benefit of such person as may be directed in writing by such parent or guardian and the receipt of such parent or guardian shall be a sufficient discharge to my executor;

(m) the receipt of the person professing to be the treasurer or other proper officer of any charity to which any legacy may be payable under this will shall be a sufficient discharge to my executor; and

(n)   to pay all necessary or proper expenses and charges from income or principal, or partly from each, in such manner as may seem equitable.

12. **I DECLARE** that any executor and/or trustee (if any) for the time being of this my will or of any codicil hereto who is a lawyer or engaged in any other profession shall be entitled to make and receive in all such charges and emoluments for business whether of an ordinary professional or other character done by him or any partner of his in relation to the administration of my estate or the execution of the trusts of this my will or any codicil hereto as he would have been entitled to make and receive in respect of such business if he had not been an executor and/or trustee.

13. **I DECLARE** that no executor or trustee of this will shall be liable for any loss not attributable to their own dishonesty or to the willful commission by them of any act known to be a breach of their duties and obligations as executor or trustee.

IN WITNESS HEREOF I have to this my Last Will and Testament, written upon this and the preceding pages, subscribed my name this _____ day of _____ 20 ___.

_____

(Signed)

Signed by the above-named testator as and for his/her Last Will and Testament in our presence, each of us being present at the same time who at his/her request and in his/her presence and in the presence of each other have hereunto subscribed our names as witnesses.

Name: _____

Signature: _____

Address: _____

_____

_____

_____

Occupation: _____

Name: _____

Signature: _____

Address: _____

_____

_____

_____

Occupation: _____

FIFTH WILL

(Married or in a civil partnership, with adult children (for wife or female partner))

Downloadable Forms

Blank copies of all this form can be downloaded from the EstateBee website. Simply login to your account or, if you don't have an account, you can create one for free.

www.estate-bee.com/login

Once logged in, go to your profile page and enter the code listed below in the 'Use Codes' tab:

FifthWillCAN21

LAST WILL AND TESTAMENT

OF

_____

THIS IS THE LAST WILL AND TESTAMENT OF _____, of _____
_____, in the province of _____.

1. I hereby **REVOKE** all former wills, codicils and other testamentary dispositions at any time heretofore made by me and declare this to be my last will.

2. [I am married to _____.]/[I am in a registered civil partnership with _____.] I have _____ child/children namely _____.

3. I appoint _____ of _____ to be executor and trustee of this my will. If this person or institution shall for any reason be unable or unwilling to act (at any time) as my executor, then I appoint _____ of _____ _____ to be executor and trustee of my will. The expression "executor" wherever used in this my will shall, unless otherwise stated, mean the person or persons from time to time acting in the office of executor and trustee of this my will, and wherever the singular or masculine are used throughout this will, the same shall be construed as meaning the plural or feminine or body corporate (and vice versa) where the context so requires.

4. I direct my executor to pay all my just debts (which are capable of enforcement against me), funeral and testamentary expenses as soon as practical after my death.

5. I give, devise, and bequeath _____ to _____
    ____ of _____ absolutely.

6. I give, devise, and bequeath _____ to _____
    ____ of _____ absolutely.

[Repeat or delete as necessary to make further specific gifts/bequests. Note you may need to renumber subsequent clauses]

7. If my husband, _____, shall survive me for a period of one month then **I GIVE, DEVISE AND BEQUEATH** all the rest, residue, and remainder of my estate of whatsoever kind and wheresoever situate to my said husband absolutely.

8. If my said husband shall predecease me or shall not survive me for the period aforesaid, I **DIRECT** that the sixth clause shall not take effect and this my will shall be construed and take effect as if the sixth clause had been wholly omitted therefrom and that the remaining clauses of this will shall take effect.

9. In so far as it may be necessary and for the avoidance of doubt, I direct that if my husband shall survive me for a period of less than one month then the income of my estate accruing from the date of my death until the date of the death of my husband shall be accumulated and form part of my residuary estate.

10. I give, devise, and bequeath all the rest, residue and remainder of my estate to _____ _____ of _____ and _____ _____ of _____ in equal shares. However, in the event that either of the above persons predecease me, then I give, devise and bequeath their share of my estate to _____ of _____.

11. In addition to all statutory powers and common law powers of executors and trustees and special powers herein conferred, my executor shall have the powers set out below:

(a) to dispose of any property or any interest therein at such times and upon such terms and conditions and in such manner as shall seem proper and to give good and sufficient instruments of transfer and to receive the proceeds of any such disposition;

(b) to invest or apply the estate or trust estate or any part thereof in any way whatsoever in which a man of ordinary prudence would invest or apply his own funds including power to borrow or lend with or without security;

(c) to purchase, manage, maintain and insure any property and to lease the same for such periods and on such terms as shall seem advantageous, and if advisable to pay for the value of any improvements made by a tenant under any such lease; to incur, extend or renew mortgage indebtedness; to make ordinary and extraordinary repairs and alterations to any building, to raze or erect buildings and to make improvements or to abandon any buildings or property;

and to make any agreement of partition of such property and to give or receive money or other property in connection therewith;

(d)   to keep property insured against such risks (if any) and for such amount as my executor shall in his/her absolute discretion think fit (but so that my executor shall not in any way be obliged to effect any insurance and shall not be liable for any failure to insure) with some insurance office of repute in the name of my executor and my executor may for such purpose pay all premiums and other costs incurred in connection with such insurance out of any money held upon the same trusts under this will or any codicil to it as such insured property (and so that the benefit of any such insurance shall be held upon the like trusts);

(e)   to exercise or sell all rights, options, powers, and privileges, and to vote in person or by proxy, in relation to any stocks, bonds or other securities, all as fully as might be done by persons owning similar property in their own right;

(f)   to assent to, oppose and participate in any reorganization, recapitalization, merger, consolidation, or similar proceeding, to deposit securities, delegate discretionary powers, pay assessments or other expenses and exchange property, all as fully as might be done by persons owning similar property in their own right;

(g)   to manage, sell, administer, liquidate, continue, or otherwise deal with any corporation, partnership or other business interest received by my trust estate as my executor deems fit;

(h)   to borrow money and pledge or mortgage any property as security therefore;

(i)   to institute, defend, settle, or compromise, by arbitration or otherwise, all claims;

(j)   to employ or retain such agents and advisors, including any firm with which any fiduciary may be affiliated, as may seem advisable and to delegate authority thereto, and to compensate them from the funds of my estate provided such compensation is reasonable in the circumstances;

k)   to settle any entitlement of any beneficiary, in part or in whole, by payment in cash or by the transfer of a specific asset or assets to the beneficiary or to the legal guardian of the beneficiary with power to require the beneficiary or any such guardian to accept such asset or assets at such value or estimate of value as my executor shall (acting reasonably) unilaterally deem fair;

(l) where my executor is authorized or required to pay a pecuniary legacy to any person who does not have the capacity to give a valid receipt for it my executor may pay the same to any parent or guardian of such person for the benefit of such person without seeing to the application of it or himself/herself apply the same for the benefit of such person as may be directed in writing by such parent or guardian and the receipt of such parent or guardian shall be a sufficient discharge to my executor;

(m) the receipt of the person professing to be the treasurer or other proper officer of any charity to which any legacy may be payable under this will shall be a sufficient discharge to my executor; and

(n) to pay all necessary or proper expenses and charges from income or principal, or partly from each, in such manner as may seem equitable.

12. **I DECLARE** that any executor and/or trustee (if any) for the time being of this my will or of any codicil hereto who is a lawyer or engaged in any other profession shall be entitled to make and receive in all such charges and emoluments for business whether of an ordinary professional or other character done by him or any partner of his in relation to the administration of my estate or the execution of the trusts of this my will or any codicil hereto as he would have been entitled to make and receive in respect of such business if he had not been an executor and/or trustee.

13. **I DECLARE** that no executor or trustee of this will shall be liable for any loss not attributable to their own dishonesty or to the willful commission by them of any act known to be a breach of their duties and obligations as executor or trustee.

IN WITNESS HEREOF I have to this my Last Will and Testament, written upon this and the preceding pages, subscribed my name this _____ day of _____ 20 ____.

_____

(Signed)

Signed by the above-named testator as and for his/her Last Will and Testament in our presence, each of us being present at the same time who at his/her request and in his/her presence and in the presence of each other have hereunto subscribed our names as witnesses.

Name: _____

Signature: _____

Address: _____

_____

_____

_____

Occupation: _____

Name: _____

Signature: _____

Address: _____

_____

_____

_____

Occupation: _____

SIXTH WILL

(Married or in a civil partnership with minor children (for husband or male partner))

Downloadable Forms

Blank copies of all this form can be downloaded from the EstateBee website. Simply login to your account or, if you don't have an account, you can create one for free.

www.estate-bee.com/login

Once logged in, go to your profile page and enter the code listed below in the 'Use Codes' tab:

SixthWillCAN21

LAST WILL AND TESTAMENT

OF

_____

THIS IS THE LAST WILL AND TESTAMENT OF _____, of _____ _____, in the province of _____.

1. I hereby **REVOKE** all former wills, codicils and other testamentary dispositions at any time heretofore made by me and declare this to be my last will.

2. [I am married to _____.]/[I am in a registered civil partnership with _____ _____.] I have _____ child/children namely _____.

3. I appoint _____ of _____ to be executor and trustee of this my will. If this person or institution shall for any reason be unable or unwilling to act (at any time) as my executor, then I appoint _____ of _____ to be executor and trustee of my will. The expression "executor" wherever used in this my will shall, unless otherwise stated, mean the person or persons from time to time acting in the office of executor and trustee of this my will, and wherever the singular or masculine are used throughout this will, the same shall be construed as meaning the plural or feminine or body corporate (and vice versa) where the context so requires.

4. I direct my executor to pay all my just debts (which are capable of enforcement against me), funeral and testamentary expenses as soon as practical after my death.

5. I appoint _____ of _____ and _____ of _____ guardians of my infant children and conservators of the estate of each of my infant children, to serve as such without bond.

6. I give, devise, and bequeath _____ to _____ of _____ absolutely.

7. I give, devise, and bequeath _____ to _____
    of _____ absolutely.

[Repeat or delete as necessary to make further specific gifts/bequests. Note you may need to renumber subsequent clauses]

8. If my wife, _____, shall survive me for a period of one month then **I GIVE, DEVISE AND BEQUEATH** all the rest, residue, and remainder of my estate of whatsoever kind and wheresoever situate to my said wife absolutely.

9. If my said wife shall predecease me or shall not survive me for the period aforesaid, I DIRECT that the sixth clause shall not take effect and this my will shall be construed and take effect as if the sixth clause had been wholly omitted therefrom and that the remaining clauses of this will shall take effect.

10. In so far as it may be necessary and for the avoidance of doubt, I direct that if my wife shall survive me for a period of less than one month then the income of my estate accruing from the date of my death until the date of the death of my wife shall be accumulated and form part of my residuary estate.

11. I give, devise, and bequeath to my executor all the rest, residue and remainder of my estate upon trust to hold the same or the proceeds of sale thereof as trustee and to divide the same among such of my children as shall survive me and reach the age of _____ years and if more than one in equal shares absolutely BUT if any child of mine dies before me or before attaining a vested interest leaving a child or children then such child or children shall on reaching the age of _____ years take per stirpes the share which his/her parent would otherwise have taken and if more than one in equal shares absolutely.

12. In addition to all statutory powers and common law powers of executors and trustees and special powers herein conferred, my executor shall have the powers set out below:

(a) to dispose of any property or any interest therein at such times and upon such terms and conditions and in such manner as shall seem proper and to give good and sufficient instruments of transfer and to receive the proceeds of any such disposition;

(b) to invest or apply the estate or trust estate or any part thereof in any way whatsoever in which a man of ordinary prudence would invest or apply his own funds including power to borrow or lend with or without security;

(c) to purchase, manage, maintain and insure any property and to lease the same for such periods and on such terms as shall seem advantageous, and if advisable to pay for the value of any improvements made by a tenant under any such lease; to incur, extend or renew mortgage indebtedness; to make ordinary and extraordinary repairs and alterations to any building, to raze or erect buildings and to make improvements or to abandon any buildings or property; and to make any agreement of partition of such property and to give or receive money or other property in connection therewith;

(d) to keep property insured against such risks (if any) and for such amount as my executor shall in his/her absolute discretion think fit (but so that my executor shall not in any way be obliged to effect any insurance and shall not be liable for any failure to insure) with some insurance office of repute in the name of my executor and my executor may for such purpose pay all premiums and other costs incurred in connection with such insurance out of any money held upon the same trusts under this will or any codicil to it as such insured property (and so that the benefit of any such insurance shall be held upon the like trusts);

(e) to exercise or sell all rights, options, powers, and privileges, and to vote in person or by proxy, in relation to any stocks, bonds or other securities, all as fully as might be done by persons owning similar property in their own right;

(f) to assent to, oppose and participate in any reorganization, recapitalization, merger, consolidation, or similar proceeding, to deposit securities, delegate discretionary powers, pay assessments or other expenses and exchange property, all as fully as might be done by persons owning similar property in their own right;

(g) to manage, sell, administer, liquidate, continue, or otherwise deal with any corporation, partnership or other business interest received by my trust estate as my executor deems fit;

(h) to borrow money and pledge or mortgage any property as security therefore;

(i) to institute, defend, settle, or compromise, by arbitration or otherwise, all claims;

(j) to employ or retain such agents and advisors, including any firm with which any fiduciary may be affiliated, as may seem advisable and to delegate authority thereto, and to compensate them from the funds of my estate provided such compensation is reasonable in the circumstances;

(k) to settle any entitlement of any beneficiary, in part or in whole, by payment in cash or by the transfer of a specific asset or assets to the beneficiary or to the legal guardian of the beneficiary with power to require the beneficiary or any such guardian to accept such asset or assets at such value or estimate of value as my executor shall (acting reasonably) unilaterally deem fair;

(l) where my executor is authorized or required to pay a pecuniary legacy to any person who does not have the capacity to give a valid receipt for it my executor may pay the same to any parent or guardian of such person for the benefit of such person without seeing to the application of it or himself/herself apply the same for the benefit of such person as may be directed in writing by such parent or guardian and the receipt of such parent or guardian shall be a sufficient discharge to my executor;

(m) the receipt of the person professing to be the treasurer or other proper officer of any charity to which any legacy may be payable under this will shall be a sufficient discharge to my executor; and

(n) to pay all necessary or proper expenses and charges from income or principal, or partly from each, in such manner as may seem equitable.

13. **I DECLARE** that any executor and/or trustee (if any) for the time being of this my will or of any codicil hereto who is a lawyer or engaged in any other profession shall be entitled to make and receive in all such charges and emoluments for business whether of an ordinary professional or other character done by him or any partner of his in relation to the administration of my estate or the execution of the trusts of this my will or any codicil hereto as he would have been entitled to make and receive in respect of such business if he had not been an executor and/or trustee.

14. **I DECLARE** that no executor or trustee of this will shall be liable for any loss not attributable to their own dishonesty or to the willful commission by them of any act known to be a breach of their duties and obligations as executor or trustee.

IN WITNESS HEREOF I have to this my Last Will and Testament, written upon this and the preceding pages, subscribed my name this _____ day of _____ 20 _____.

Name: _____

Signature: _____

Address: _____

_____

_____

_____

Occupation: _____

Name: _____

Signature: _____

Address: _____

_____

_____

_____

Occupation: _____

SEVENTH WILL

(Married or in a civil partnership with minor children (for wife or female partner))

Downloadable Forms

Blank copies of all this form can be downloaded from the EstateBee website. Simply login to your account or, if you don't have an account, you can create one for free.

www.estate-bee.com/login

Once logged in, go to your profile page and enter the code listed below in the 'Use Codes' tab:

SeventhWillCAN21

LAST WILL AND TESTAMENT

OF

_____

THIS IS THE LAST WILL AND TESTAMENT OF _____, of _____ _____, in the province of _____.

1. I hereby **REVOKE** all former wills, codicils and other testamentary dispositions at any time heretofore made by me and declare this to be my last will.

2. [I am married to _____.]/[I am in a registered civil partnership with _____ _____.] I have _____ child/children namely _____.

3. I appoint _____ of _____ to be executor and trustee of this my will. If this person or institution shall for any reason be unable or unwilling to act (at any time) as my executor, then I appoint _____ of _____ to be executor and trustee of my will. The expression "executor" wherever used in this my will shall, unless otherwise stated, mean the person or persons from time to time acting in the office of executor and trustee of this my will, and wherever the singular or masculine are used throughout this will, the same shall be construed as meaning the plural or feminine or body corporate (and vice versa) where the context so requires.

4. I direct my executor to pay all my just debts (which are capable of enforcement against me), funeral and testamentary expenses as soon as practical after my death.

5. I appoint _____ of _____ and _____ of _____ guardians of my infant children and conservators of the estate of each of my infant children, to serve as such without bond.

6. I give, devise, and bequeath _____ to _____ of _____ absolutely.

7. I give, devise, and bequeath _____ to _____
    of _____ absolutely.

[Repeat or delete as necessary to make further specific gifts/bequests. Note you may need to renumber subsequent clauses]

8. If my husband, _____, shall survive me for a period of one month then **I GIVE, DEVISE AND BEQUEATH** all the rest, residue, and remainder of my estate of whatsoever kind and wheresoever situate to my said husband absolutely.

9. If my said husband shall predecease me or shall not survive me for the period aforesaid, I DIRECT that the sixth clause shall not take effect and this my will shall be construed and take effect as if the sixth clause had been wholly omitted therefrom and that the remaining clauses of this will shall take effect.

10. In so far as it may be necessary and for the avoidance of doubt, I direct that if my husband shall survive me for a period of less than one month then the income of my estate accruing from the date of my death until the date of the death of my husband shall be accumulated and form part of my residuary estate.

11. I give, devise, and bequeath to my executor all the rest, residue and remainder of my estate upon trust to hold the same or the proceeds of sale thereof as trustee and to divide the same among such of my children as shall survive me and reach the age of _____ years and if more than one in equal shares absolutely BUT if any child of mine dies before me or before attaining a vested interest leaving a child or children then such child or children shall on reaching the age of _____ years take per stirpes the share which his/her parent would otherwise have taken and if more than one in equal shares absolutely.

12. In addition to all statutory powers and common law powers of executors and trustees and special powers herein conferred, my executor shall have the powers set out below:

(a) to dispose of any property or any interest therein at such times and upon such terms and conditions and in such manner as shall seem proper and to give good and sufficient instruments of transfer and to receive the proceeds of any such disposition;

(b)   to invest or apply the estate or trust estate or any part thereof in any way whatsoever in which a man of ordinary prudence would invest or apply his own funds including power to borrow or lend with or without security;

(c)   to purchase, manage, maintain and insure any property and to lease the same for such periods and on such terms as shall seem advantageous, and if advisable to pay for the value of any improvements made by a tenant under any such lease; to incur, extend or renew mortgage indebtedness; to make ordinary and extraordinary repairs and alterations to any building, to raze or erect buildings and to make improvements or to abandon any buildings or property; and to make any agreement of partition of such property and to give or receive money or other property in connection therewith;

(d)   to keep property insured against such risks (if any) and for such amount as my executor shall in his/her absolute discretion think fit (but so that my executor shall not in any way be obliged to effect any insurance and shall not be liable for any failure to insure) with some insurance office of repute in the name of my executor and my executor may for such purpose pay all premiums and other costs incurred in connection with such insurance out of any money held upon the same trusts under this will or any codicil to it as such insured property (and so that the benefit of any such insurance shall be held upon the like trusts);

(e)   to exercise or sell all rights, options, powers, and privileges, and to vote in person or by proxy, in relation to any stocks, bonds or other securities, all as fully as might be done by persons owning similar property in their own right;

(f)   to assent to, oppose and participate in any reorganization, recapitalization, merger, consolidation, or similar proceeding, to deposit securities, delegate discretionary powers, pay assessments or other expenses and exchange property, all as fully as might be done by persons owning similar property in their own right;

(g)   to manage, sell, administer, liquidate, continue, or otherwise deal with any corporation, partnership or other business interest received by my trust estate as my executor deems fit;

(h)   to borrow money and pledge or mortgage any property as security therefore;

(i)   to institute, defend, settle, or compromise, by arbitration or otherwise, all claims;

(j)   to employ or retain such agents and advisors, including any firm with which any fiduciary may be affiliated, as may seem advisable and to delegate authority thereto, and to compensate them from the funds of my estate provided such compensation is reasonable in the circumstances;

(k)   to settle any entitlement of any beneficiary, in part or in whole, by payment in cash or by the transfer of a specific asset or assets to the beneficiary or to the legal guardian of the beneficiary with power to require the beneficiary or any such guardian to accept such asset or assets at such value or estimate of value as my executor shall (acting reasonably) unilaterally deem fair;

(l)   where my executor is authorized or required to pay a pecuniary legacy to any person who does not have the capacity to give a valid receipt for it my executor may pay the same to any parent or guardian of such person for the benefit of such person without seeing to the application of it or himself/herself apply the same for the benefit of such person as may be directed in writing by such parent or guardian and the receipt of such parent or guardian shall be a sufficient discharge to my executor;

(m) the receipt of the person professing to be the treasurer or other proper officer of any charity to which any legacy may be payable under this will shall be a sufficient discharge to my executor; and

(n)   to pay all necessary or proper expenses and charges from income or principal, or partly from each, in such manner as may seem equitable.

13.   **I DECLARE** that any executor and/or trustee (if any) for the time being of this my will or of any codicil hereto who is a lawyer or engaged in any other profession shall be entitled to make and receive in all such charges and emoluments for business whether of an ordinary professional or other character done by him or any partner of his in relation to the administration of my estate or the execution of the trusts of this my will or any codicil hereto as he would have been entitled to make and receive in respect of such business if he had not been an executor and/or trustee.

14.   **I DECLARE** that no executor or trustee of this will shall be liable for any loss not attributable to their own dishonesty or to the willful commission by them of any act known to be a breach of their duties and obligations as executor or trustee.

IN WITNESS HEREOF I have to this my Last Will and Testament, written upon this and the preceding pages, subscribed my name this _____ day of _____ 20 _____.

_____

(Signed)

Signed by the above-named testator as and for his/her Last Will and Testament in our presence, each of us being present at the same time who at his/her request and in his/her presence and in the presence of each other have hereunto subscribed our names as witnesses.

Name: _____

Signature: _____

Address: _____

_____

_____

_____

Occupation: _____

Name: _____

Signature: _____

Address: _____

_____

_____

_____

Occupation: _____

EIGHTH WILL

(Person who is married or in a civil partnership with no children (for husband/male partner))

Downloadable Forms

Blank copies of all this form can be downloaded from the EstateBee website. Simply login to your account or, if you don't have an account, you can create one for free.

www.estate-bee.com/login

Once logged in, go to your profile page and enter the code listed below in the 'Use Codes' tab:

EighthWillCAN21

LAST WILL AND TESTAMENT

OF

_____

THIS IS THE LAST WILL AND TESTAMENT OF _____, of _____
_____, County _____.

1. I hereby **REVOKE** all former wills, codicils and other testamentary dispositions at any time heretofore made by me and declare this to be my last will.

2. [I am married to _____.]/ [I am in a registered civil partnership with _____.] I do not have any living children.

3. I appoint _____ of _____ to be executor and trustee of this my will. If this person or institution shall for any reason be unable or unwilling to act (at any time) as my executor, then I appoint _____ of ____ _____ to be executor and trustee of my will. The expression "executor" wherever used in this my will shall, unless otherwise stated, mean the person or persons from time to time acting in the office of executor and trustee of this my will, and wherever the singular or masculine are used throughout this will, the same shall be construed as meaning the plural or feminine or body corporate (and vice versa) where the context so requires.

4. I direct my executor to pay all my just debts (which are capable of enforcement against me), funeral and testamentary expenses as soon as practical after my death.

5. I give, devise, and bequeath _____ to _____ of _____ absolutely.

6. I give, devise, and bequeath _____ to _____ of _____ absolutely.

[Repeat or delete as necessary to make further specific gifts/bequests. Note you may need to renumber subsequent clauses]

7. If my [wife]/[partner], _____, shall survive me for a period of one month then **I GIVE, DEVISE AND BEQUEATH** all the rest, residue, and remainder of my estate of whatsoever kind and wheresoever situate to my said [wife]/[partner] absolutely.

8. If my said [wife]/[partner] shall predecease me or shall not survive me for the period aforesaid **I DIRECT** that the previous clause shall not take effect and this my will shall be construed and take effect as if the previous clause had been wholly omitted therefrom and that the remaining clauses of this will shall take effect.

9. In so far as it may be necessary and for the avoidance of doubt, I direct that if my [wife]/[partner] shall survive me for a period of less than one month then the income of my estate accruing from the date of my death until the date of the death of my [wife]/[partner] shall be accumulated and form part of my residuary estate.

10. I give, devise, and bequeath all the rest, residue and remainder of my estate to _____ _____ of _____ and _____ of ___ _____ in equal shares. However, in the event that either of the above persons predeceases me, then I give, devise and bequeath their share of my estate to _____ _____ of _____.

11. In addition to all statutory powers and common law powers of executors and trustees and special powers herein conferred, my Executor shall have the powers set out below:

(a) to dispose of any property or any interest therein at such times and upon such terms and conditions and in such manner as shall seem proper and to give good and sufficient instruments of transfer and to receive the proceeds of any such disposition;

(b) to invest or apply the estate or trust estate or any part thereof in any way whatsoever in which a man of ordinary prudence would invest or apply his own funds including power to borrow or lend with or without security;

(c) to purchase, manage, maintain and insure any property and to lease the same for such periods and on such terms as shall seem advantageous, and if advisable to pay for the value of any improvements made by a tenant under any such lease; to incur, extend or renew mortgage indebtedness; to make ordinary and extraordinary repairs and alterations to any building, to raze or erect buildings and to make improvements or to abandon any buildings or property; and to make any agreement of partition of such property and to give or receive money or other property in connection therewith;

(d)   to keep property insured against such risks (if any) and for such amount as my executor shall in his/her absolute discretion think fit (but so that my executor shall not in any way be obliged to effect any insurance and shall not be liable for any failure to insure) with some insurance office of repute in the name of my executor and my executor may for such purpose pay all premiums and other costs incurred in connection with such insurance out of any money held upon the same trusts under this will or any codicil to it as such insured property (and so that the benefit of any such insurance shall be held upon the like trusts);

(e)   to exercise or sell all rights, options, powers, and privileges, and to vote in person or by proxy, in relation to any stocks, bonds or other securities, all as fully as might be done by persons owning similar property in their own right;

(f)   to assent to, oppose and participate in any reorganization, recapitalization, merger, consolidation, or similar proceeding, to deposit securities, delegate discretionary powers, pay assessments or other expenses and exchange property, all as fully as might be done by persons owning similar property in their own right;

(g)   to manage, sell, administer, liquidate, continue, or otherwise deal with any corporation, partnership or other business interest received by my trust estate as my executor deems fit;

(h)   to borrow money and pledge or mortgage any property as security therefore;

(i)   to institute, defend, settle, or compromise, by arbitration or otherwise, all claims;

(j)   to employ or retain such agents and advisors, including any firm with which any fiduciary may be affiliated, as may seem advisable and to delegate authority thereto, and to compensate them from the funds of my estate provided such compensation is reasonable in the circumstances;

(k) to settle any entitlement of any beneficiary, in part or in whole, by payment in cash or by the transfer of a specific asset or assets to the beneficiary or to the legal guardian of the beneficiary with power to require the beneficiary or any such guardian to accept such asset or assets at such value or estimate of value as my executor shall (acting reasonably) unilaterally deem fair;

(l) where my executor is authorized or required to pay a pecuniary legacy to any person who does not have the capacity to give a valid receipt for it my executor may pay the same to any parent or guardian of such person for the benefit of such person without seeing to the application of it or himself/herself apply the same for the benefit of such person as may be directed in writing by such parent or guardian and the receipt of such parent or guardian shall be a sufficient discharge to my executor;

(m) the receipt of the person professing to be the treasurer or other proper officer of any charity to which any legacy may be payable under this will shall be a sufficient discharge to my executor; and

(n) to pay all necessary or proper expenses and charges from income or principal, or partly from each, in such manner as may seem equitable.

12. **I DECLARE** that any executor and/or trustee (if any) for the time being of this my will or of any codicil hereto who is a lawyer or engaged in any other profession shall be entitled to make and receive in all such charges and emoluments for business whether of an ordinary professional or other character done by him or any partner of his in relation to the administration of my estate or the execution of the trusts of this my will or any codicil hereto as he would have been entitled to make and receive in respect of such business if he had not been an executor and/or trustee.

13. **I DECLARE** that no executor or trustee of this will shall be liable for any loss not attributable to their own dishonesty or to the willful commission by them of any act known to be a breach of their duties and obligations as executor or trustee.

14. **I DECLARE** that no advancements shall be brought into account in the distribution of my estate.

IN WITNESS HEREOF, I have hereunto signed my name this _____ day of _____ _____ 20 _____.

_____
(Signed)

Signed by the above-named testator as and for his/her Last Will and Testament in our presence, each of us being present at the same time who at his/her request and in his/her presence and in the presence of each other have hereunto subscribed our names as witnesses.

Name: _____

Signature: _____

Address: _____

_____

_____

_____

Occupation: _____

Name: _____

Signature: _____

Address: _____

_____

_____

_____

Occupation: _____

NINTH WILL

(Person who is married or in a civil partnership, with no children (for wife or female partner)

Downloadable Forms

Blank copies of all this form can be downloaded from the EstateBee website.
Simply login to your account or, if you don't have an account, you can create one for free.

www.estate-bee.com/login

Once logged in, go to your profile page and enter the code listed below in the 'Use Codes' tab:

NinthWillCAN21

LAST WILL AND TESTAMENT

OF

_____

THIS IS THE LAST WILL AND TESTAMENT OF _____, of _____
_____, County _____.

1. I hereby **REVOKE** all former wills, codicils and other testamentary dispositions at any time heretofore made by me and declare this to be my last will.

2. [I am married to _____.]/ [I am in a registered civil partnership with _____.] I do not have any living children.

3. I appoint _____ of _____ to be executor and trustee of this my will. If this person or institution shall for any reason be unable or unwilling to act (at any time) as my executor, then I appoint _____ of _____ to be executor and trustee of my will. The expression "executor" wherever used in this my will shall, unless otherwise stated, mean the person or persons from time to time acting in the office of executor and trustee of this my will, and wherever the singular or masculine are used throughout this will, the same shall be construed as meaning the plural or feminine or body corporate (and vice versa) where the context so requires.

4. I direct my executor to pay all my just debts (which are capable of enforcement against me), funeral and testamentary expenses as soon as practical after my death.

5. I give, devise, and bequeath _____ to _____
_____ of _____.

6. I give, devise, and bequeath _____ to _____
_____ of _____.

[Repeat or delete as necessary to make further specific gifts/bequests. Note you may need to renumber subsequent clauses]

7. If my [husband]/[partner], _____, shall survive me for a period of one month then I **GIVE, DEVISE AND BEQUEATH** all the rest, residue, and remainder of my estate of whatsoever kind and wheresoever situate to my said [husband]/[partner] absolutely.

8. If my said [husband]/[partner] shall predecease me or shall not survive me for the period aforesaid I **DIRECT** that the previous clause shall not take effect and this my will shall be construed and take effect as if the previous clause had been wholly omitted therefrom and that the remaining clauses of this will shall take effect.

9. In so far as it may be necessary and for the avoidance of doubt, I direct that if my [husband]/[partner] shall survive me for a period of less than one month then the income of my estate accruing from the date of my death until the date of the death of my [husband]/[partner] shall be accumulated and form part of my residuary estate.

10. I give, devise, and bequeath all the rest, residue and remainder of my estate to _____ _____ of _____ and _____ _____ of _____ equal shares. However, in the event that either of the above persons predeceases me, then I give, devise and bequeath their share of my estate to _____ of _____.

11. In addition to all statutory powers and common law powers of executors and trustees and special powers herein conferred, my Executor shall have the powers set out below:

a) to dispose of any property or any interest therein at such times and upon such terms and conditions and in such manner as shall seem proper and to give good and sufficient instruments of transfer and to receive the proceeds of any such disposition;

(b) to invest or apply the estate or trust estate or any part thereof in any way whatsoever in which a man of ordinary prudence would invest or apply his own funds including power to borrow or lend with or without security;

(c) to purchase, manage, maintain and insure any property and to lease the same for such periods and on such terms as shall seem advantageous, and if advisable to pay for the value of any improvements made by a tenant under any such lease; to incur, extend or renew mortgage indebtedness; to make ordinary and extraordinary repairs and alterations to any building, to raze or erect buildings and to make improvements or to abandon any buildings or property; and to make any agreement of partition of such property and to give or receive money or other property in connection therewith;

(d) to keep property insured against such risks (if any) and for such amount as my executor shall in his/her absolute discretion think fit (but so that my executor shall not in any way be obliged to effect any insurance and shall not be liable for any failure to insure) with some insurance office of repute in the name of my executor and my executor may for such purpose pay all premiums and other costs incurred in connection with such insurance out of any money held upon the same trusts under this will or any codicil to it as such insured property (and so that the benefit of any such insurance shall be held upon the like trusts);

(e) to exercise or sell all rights, options, powers, and privileges, and to vote in person or by proxy, in relation to any stocks, bonds or other securities, all as fully as might be done by persons owning similar property in their own right;

(f) to assent to, oppose and participate in any reorganization, recapitalization, merger, consolidation, or similar proceeding, to deposit securities, delegate discretionary powers, pay assessments or other expenses and exchange property, all as fully as might be done by persons owning similar property in their own right;

(g) to manage, sell, administer, liquidate, continue, or otherwise deal with any corporation, partnership or other business interest received by my trust estate as my executor deems fit;

(h) to borrow money and pledge or mortgage any property as security therefore;

(i) to institute, defend, settle, or compromise, by arbitration or otherwise, all claims;

(j) to employ or retain such agents and advisors, including any firm with which any fiduciary may be affiliated, as may seem advisable and to delegate authority thereto, and to compensate them from the funds of my estate provided such compensation is reasonable in the circumstances;

(k) to settle any entitlement of any beneficiary, in part or in whole, by payment in cash or by the transfer of a specific asset or assets to the beneficiary or to the legal guardian of the beneficiary with power to require the beneficiary or any such guardian to accept such asset or assets at such value or estimate of value as my executor shall (acting reasonably) unilaterally deem fair;

(l)   where my executor is authorized or required to pay a pecuniary legacy to any person who does not have the capacity to give a valid receipt for it my executor may pay the same to any parent or guardian of such person for the benefit of such person without seeing to the application of it or himself/herself apply the same for the benefit of such person as may be directed in writing by such parent or guardian and the receipt of such parent or guardian shall be a sufficient discharge to my executor;

(m)   the receipt of the person professing to be the treasurer or other proper officer of any charity to which any legacy may be payable under this will shall be a sufficient discharge to my executor; and

(n)   to pay all necessary or proper expenses and charges from income or principal, or partly from each, in such manner as may seem equitable.

13.   **I DECLARE** that any executor and/or trustee (if any) for the time being of this my will or of any codicil hereto who is a lawyer or engaged in any other profession shall be entitled to make and receive in all such charges and emoluments for business whether of an ordinary professional or other character done by him or any partner of his in relation to the administration of my estate or the execution of the trusts of this my will or any codicil hereto as he would have been entitled to make and receive in respect of such business if he had not been an executor and/or trustee.

13.   **I DECLARE** that no executor or trustee of this will shall be liable for any loss not attributable to their own dishonesty or to the willful commission by them of any act known to be a breach of their duties and obligations as executor or trustee.

14.   I DECLARE that no advancements shall be brought into account in the distribution of my estate.

IN WITNESS HEREOF, I have hereunto signed my name this _____ day of _____ 20 __.

_____

(Signed)

Signed by the above-named testator as and for his/her Last Will and Testament in our presence, each of us being present at the same time who at his/her request and in his/her presence and in the presence of each other have hereunto subscribed our names as witnesses.

Name: _____

Signature: _____

Address: _____

_____

_____

_____

Occupation: _____

Name: _____

Signature: _____

Address: _____

_____

_____

_____

Occupation: _____

Appendix 4

General Instructions for Completing Your Will

Appendix 4

General Instructions for Completing your Will

1. Carefully read all the instructions below and select the will from Appendix 3 which is most suitable to your circumstances.

2. Carefully consider who will act as your executors, trustees, witnesses and guardians (if any). Carefully consider who will be the proposed beneficiaries. When inputting the details in your will, you must be as specific as possible and avoid broad statements such as "my friends".

3. Print out the will form which you intend using and complete it neatly using a pen or carefully edit the text version of the form (that is available to you to download) on your computer.

    The will should be completed in accordance with the special instructions in Appendix 5. Do not leave any blank spaces.

4. Arrange for two witnesses to be present. Date and sign your will in the presence of the two witnesses. Then have each of your two witnesses sign and complete the details (name, signature, address, and occupation) on the final page of your will in your presence and in the presence of the other witness. In Quebec, each of the testator and witnesses also need to initial the bottom right side of each page.

Appendix 5

Specific Instructions for Completing Your Will

Appendix 5

Specific Instructions for Completing Your Will

Instructions for completion of First Will document

1. Fill in your name in the space provided in the title "last will and testament of ____".

2. Fill in your name and address in the space provided in the first paragraph.

3. In clause 3, fill in the name and address of your executor and the name and address of your alternate executor.**

4. In clauses 5 and 6, fill in the names and addresses of the proposed beneficiary of each specific gift and details of that specific gift. Add or delete gift clauses as you require but remember to re-number the subsequent clause numbers as appropriate.

5. In clause 7, fill in the name and address of the sole beneficiary of your estate and the name and address of your alternate beneficiary.

6. Now Go to Number 4 in the General Instructions (Appendix 4).

Instructions for completion of Second Will document

1. Fill in your name in the space provided in the title "last will and testament of ____".

2. Fill in your name and address in the space provided in the first paragraph.

3. In clause 3, fill in the name and address of your executor and the name and address of your alternate executor.**

4. In clauses 5 and 6, fill in the names and addresses of the proposed beneficiary of each specific gift and details of that specific gift. Add or delete gift clauses as you require but remember to re-number the subsequent clause numbers as appropriate.

5. In clause 7, fill in the name and address of the two beneficiaries of your estate and the name and address of your alternate beneficiary.*

6. Now Go to Number 4 in the General Instructions (Appendix 4).

Instructions for completion of Third Will document

1. Fill in your name in the space provided in the title "last will and testament of ____".

2. Fill in your name and address in the space provided in the first paragraph.

3. In clause 2, specify the number of children you have and the names of each child.

4. In clause 3, fill in the name and address of your executor and the name and address of your alternate executor.**

5. In clause 5, fill in the name and address of the each of the two proposed guardians of your minor children.

6. In clauses 6 and 7, fill in the names and addresses of the proposed beneficiary of each specific gift and details of that specific gift. Add or delete gift clauses as you require but remember to re-number the subsequent clause numbers as appropriate.

7. In clause 8, fill in the age at which your children should receive their inheritance, for example, eighteen or twenty-one. This will need to be inserted in two places in this clause.

8. Now Go to Number 4 in the General Instructions (Appendix 4).

Instructions for completion of Fourth & Fifth Will documents

1. Fill in your name in the space provided in the title "last will and testament of ____".

2. Fill in your name and address in the space provided in the first paragraph.

3. In clause 2, enter the name of your spouse or partner (and delete the section in square brackets regarding the spouse or partner which is not relevant to your situation) and then specify the number of children you have and the names of each child. Remember to move all square brackets.

4. In clause 3, fill in the name and address of your executor and the name and address of your alternate executor.**

5. In clauses 5 and 6, fill in the names and addresses of the proposed beneficiary of each specific gift and details of that specific gift. Add or delete gift clauses as you require but remember to re-number the subsequent clause numbers as appropriate.

6. In clause 7, fill in the name of your spouse or partner and delete the part of the text "[husband]/[partner]" which is not relevant to your situation – so that the text only reads either husband or partner. You will need to make this deletion in two places in this clause. Remember to remove all square brackets.

7. In clause 8, delete the part of the text "[husband]/[partner]" which is not relevant to your situation – so that the text only reads either husband or partner. You will need to make this deletion in one place only in this clause. Remember to remove all square brackets.

8. In clause 9, delete the part of the text "[husband]/[partner]" which is not relevant to your situation – so that the text only reads either husband or partner. You will need to make this deletion in two places in this clause. Remember to remove all square brackets.

9. In clause 10, fill in the name and address of each of the beneficiaries of your estate who will benefit should your spouse predecease you or fail to survive you by a period of 30 days. You will also need to enter the name of an alternate beneficiary.*

10. Now Go to Number 4 in the General Instructions (Appendix 4).

Instructions for completion of Sixth and Seventh Will documents

1.   Fill in your name in the space provided in the title "last will and testament of ____".

2.   Fill in your name and address in the space provided in the first paragraph.

3.   In clause 2, enter the name of your spouse or partner (and delete the section in square brackets regarding the spouse or partner which is not relevant to your situation) and then specify the number of children you have and the names of each child. Remember to move all square brackets.

4.   In clause 3, fill in the name and address of your executor and the name and address of your alternate executor.**

5.   In clause 5, fill in the names and addresses of the proposed guardians of your infant children.

6.   In clauses 6 and 7, fill in the names and addresses of the proposed beneficiary of each specific gift and details of that specific gift. Add or delete gift clauses as you require but remember to re-number the subsequent clause numbers as appropriate.

7.   In clause 8, fill in the name of your spouse or partner and delete the part of the text "[husband]/[partner]" which is not relevant to your situation – so that the text only reads either husband or partner. You will need to make this deletion in two places in this clause. Remember to remove all square brackets.

8.   In clause 9, delete the part of the text "[husband]/[partner]" which is not relevant to your situation – so that the text only reads either husband or partner. You will need to make this deletion in one place only in this clause. Remember to remove all square brackets.

9.   In clause 10, delete the part of the text "[husband]/[partner]" which is not relevant to your situation – so that the text only reads either husband or partner. You will need to make this

deletion in two places in this clause. Remember to remove all square brackets.

10. In clause 11, fill in the age at which your children should receive their inheritance, for example, eighteen or twenty-one.

11. Now Go to Number 4 in the General Instructions (Appendix 4).

Instructions for completion of Eighth & Ninth Will documents

1. Fill in your name in the space provided in the title "last will and testament of ____".

2. Fill in your name and address in the space provided in the first paragraph.

3. In clause 2, enter the name of your spouse or partner (and delete the section in square brackets regarding the spouse or partner which is not relevant to your situation). Delete all square brackets.

4. In clause 3, fill in the name and address of your executor and the name and address of your alternate executor.**

5. In clauses 5 and 6, fill in the names and addresses of the proposed beneficiary of each specific gift and details of that specific gift. Add or delete gift clauses as you require but remember to re-number the subsequent clause numbers as appropriate.

6. In clause 7, fill in the name of your spouse or partner and delete the part of the text "[husband/wife]/[partner]" which is not relevant to your situation – so that the text only reads either husband or partner. You will need to make this deletion in two places in this clause. Remember to remove all square brackets.

7. In clause 8, delete the part of the text "[husband/wife]/[partner]" which is not relevant to your situation – so that the text only reads either husband or partner. You will need to make this deletion in one place only in this clause. Remember to remove all square brackets.

8. In clause 9, delete the part of the text "[husband/wife]/[partner]" which is not relevant to your situation – so that the text only reads either husband or partner. You will need to make this deletion in two places in this clause. Remember to remove all square brackets.

9. In clause 10, fill in the name and address of each of the beneficiaries of your estate who will benefit should your spouse predecease you or fail to survive you by a period of 30 days. You will also need to enter the name of an alternate beneficiary.*

10. Now Go to Number 4 in the General Instructions (Appendix 4).

Notes:

* You can also name more than two alternate beneficiaries and state that each will have a specific percentage of the residuary estate. However, in making any amendments to the residuary clause, be sure to state what you want in very specific terms.

**Executors: Note, you may wish to appoint two executors (and two substitute executors) to act jointly. In this case, simply add the name and address of the second executor such that the sentence specifies that you appoint Person 1 and Person 2 to act as executors.

Appendix 6

Additional Clauses That You May Wish to Add....

Appointing an alternate beneficiary for a specific gift

I give, devise, and bequeath _____ to _____ of __
_____ absolutely. If this person is unable or unwilling to accept this gift
(for any reason) then I give same to _____ of _____
_____ absolutely.

Releasing someone from a debt

I release and forgive _____ of _____ and should he/she
predecease me his/her executors and estate from all debt due to me at the date of my death and
from all interest due in respect thereof.

Or

I release and forgive _____ of _____ and should he/she
predecease me his/her personal representatives and estate from the debt of _____ and from
all interest due in respect thereof.

Nominating assets to be sold to pay debts

I direct my executors to pay my enforceable unsecured debts and funeral expenses, the expenses
of my last illness, and the expenses of administering my estate using the following asset(s):- _____
_____.

Burial clause

I direct that my executors should bury me at [insert name and address of cemetery].

Cremation clause

I desire that my body be cremated in the crematorium at [insert name and address of crematorium]. I further direct that my ashes be [insert details of what should be done with your ashes].

Revocation clause – where a foreign will has been made

I hereby revoke all former Wills, codicils and other testamentary dispositions at any time heretofore made by me dealing with my estate in Canada only and declare this to be my last Will. This revocation does not affect any other Will, codicil or other testamentary disposition I may previously have made dealing with my property outside Canada.

Manufactured by Amazon.ca
Bolton, ON

34368690R00098